Thomas George Gentry

The House Sparrow at Home and Abroad

With some Concluding Remarks Upon its Usefulness, and Copious ....

Thomas George Gentry

The House Sparrow at Home and Abroad
With some Concluding Remarks Upon its Usefulness, and Copious ....

ISBN/EAN: 9783337139001

Printed in Europe, USA, Canada, Australia, Japan

Cover: Foto ©Andreas Hilbeck / pixelio.de

More available books at **www.hansebooks.com**

THE
HOUSE SPARROW
AT
HOME AND ABROAD,

WITH SOME

CONCLUDING REMARKS UPON ITS USEFULNESS,

AND

COPIOUS REFERENCES TO THE LITERATURE OF THE SUBJECT.

BY

THOMAS G. GENTRY,

AUTHOR OF LIFE-HISTORIES OF BIRDS OF EASTERN PENNSYLVANIA,
MEMBER OF THE PHILADELPHIA ACADEMY OF NATURAL SCIENCES,
AND CORRESPONDING MEMBER OF NUTTALL ORNITHOLOGICAL
CLUB, DAVENPORT ACADEMY OF NATURAL SCIENCES,
AND CANADIAN ENTOMOLOGICAL SOCIETY.

PHILADELPHIA:
CLAXTON, REMSEN, AND HAFFELFINGER.
1878.

Entered according to the Act of Congress, in the year 1878, by

THOMAS G. GENTRY,

in the Office of the Librarian of Congress. All rights reserved.

PHILADELPHIA:
COLLINS, PRINTER.
705 Jayne Street.

PREFACE.

In offering this little volume to the public, the author feels confident that it will meet with a cordial reception from those who have neither the leisure nor the patience to make such investigations as a work like the present requires. In view of the many heated discussions which the sparrow has produced in this country, tending to show its general usefulness, or wholesale destructiveness, a careful and critical survey of its life-history, detailing the minutest particulars thereof, cannot fail to awaken attention and to command respect. A desire to know the subject in all its bearings, must certainly be of paramount importance. Agriculturists and fruit-growers, mainly of all others, will certainly reap the first fruits of such knowledge. The facts, which the writer has gleaned from various fields of observation, but largely from his own, at infinite pains and expense, subserve, in the highest degree, the interests of humanity, and should not be carelessly set aside or lightly considered.

With the disappearance of our highly insectivorous native species before the rapid and insolent advances of their hardy foreign brother, and the consequent multiplication of insect foes, must come the destruction of vegetation and the entailment of untold misery upon man and beast. The sparrow itself, by reason of its almost exclusive grain-eating habits, will assist in bringing about this much-to-be-regretted condition of things. He must be a fool who can close his eyes to the fact. Wherever we turn, evidence of its baneful influence confronts our vision. We cannot escape it. Can it be said, therefore, that a history of this bane of our avi-fauna, and curse of man, is labor bestowed upon a worthless object, is time sacrificed for nothing? I know it will be affirmed by some, even if it has not been already, that the sparrow is not deserving of the attention bestowed upon it. In reply the writer would say that his only plea for writing its history is that a more general knowledge of its odious practices, which are manifold, shall be brought before the masses, particularly that class of hard-working men, the tillers of the soil, and the growers of vegetables, upon whom the professional man and the brawny mechanic depend for many of the essential articles of life. Further, to awaken attention to the growing evil, in the confident expectation that it may be instrumental in the adoption of practicable means for getting rid of the intolerable nuisance.

With the hope that this little book may accomplish the object for which it is designed, and be instrumental in the production of much invaluable good, the author sends it forth upon its mission of kindness and mercy, with his best wishes for its success.

THOMAS G. GENTRY.

GERMANTOWN, Dec. 6, 1877,
55 Sharpnack Street.

CONTENTS.

	PAGE
INTRODUCTION	9
The Sparrow in Europe	11
The Sparrow in America	33
Evidence, both Positive and Negative, of the Sparrow's Usefulness in America	74
Concluding Remarks	96
Appendix	113

THE HOUSE SPARROW.

INTRODUCTION.

In commencing the history of the European House Sparrow, which I have selected for the title of a work, it cannot be considered out of place to introduce the subject by a few remarks upon its position in a system of classification. What I shall have to say under this head will be mainly derived from the investigations and studies of Dr. Coues. According to that author, the subject under consideration must be referred to

Subclass I.—**AVES AËREÆ**, or Insessores, Aërial Birds, or Perchers.

Of the three primary divisions constituting the class *Aves*, the foregoing ranks as first in importance, and highest in position. It embraces all existing species of birds down to the *Gallinæ*, or gallinaceous birds. A full definition of its external characters, in a work like the present, would be entirely unnecessary. Suffice it to say that, with rare exceptions, the toes occupy the same plane, and touch the same support throughout, thus adapting them for grasping, or perching. The members of this extensive group are now generally placed in *five* orders, of which the first is the

ORDER **Passeres.** Perchers proper.

The low insertion of the hind toe and its length; its great power of opposibility to the front toes; and the superior mobility of the same, which is secured by the separation of its principal muscle from that which flexes the other toes collectively, perfectly adapt the feet for grasping. The hind toe is always present, and is never directed anteriorly, or laterally. The feet are never zygodactyl, esyndactyle, nor semipalmate, although the anterior toes, for a part or the entire length of the basal joints, are usually immovably joined to each other. For further particulars, the reader should examine some standard work upon classification.

The species belonging to this order are the typical *Insessores*, and represent the highest grade of development, as well as the most complex of the class. They possess high physical irritability, the result of a rapid respiration and circulation; of all birds, they consume the most oxygen, and live the fastest.

The *Passeres* comprise the great majority of birds. They are separated into two groups, ordinarily designated suborders, from the structure of the inferior larynx. In one, this organ is a complicated muscular vocal apparatus; while in the other, it is less developed, rudimentary, or lacking.

Suborder OSCINES. Singing Birds.

The above constitutes the higher of the two suborders previously referred to; comprising species, which possess a more or less complicated vocal apparatus, consisting of five sets of muscles; but many of them are unable to

INTRODUCTION.   11

sing. Ornithologists are not agreed as to which of the
numerous Oscine families should occupy the head of the
series; but Dr. Coues inclines to the opinion that some
member of this family with the possession of nine primaries—as the finches or tanagers—will eventually assume the leading place. The *Turdidæ*, or Thrushes,
in accordance with usage, occupy this position.

Family FRINGILLIDÆ. Finches, etc.

The *Fringillidæ* are the most extensive group in ornithology, representing, in round numbers, 500 current
species in about 100 genera. This family represents
more particularly what used to be designated "conirostral" birds. The bill of these birds approaches nearest
to the ideal cone, and unites great strength with deli-
cacy of touch.

The cone is sometimes nearly expressed, but frequently turgid and conoidal; convex in most directions,
and so constructed as to become concave in some of its
outlines. The nostrils are usually exposed, but in many
northern genera the base of the bill is furnished with a
ruff and two tufts of antrorse feathers, which more or
less conceal the opening; the cutting edges of bill are
slightly notched, but otherwise plain; a few inconspicuous bristles about rictus; ordinarily, somewhat lacking;
in some, highly developed. The wings are composed of
nine developed primaries, variable in size; the tail is
variable, but always composed of twelve rectrices; feet
scutellate in front, and covered on side with an un-
divided plate, which produces a sharp ridge posteriorly.

The most tangible character of this group is the an-
gulation of the commissure; this character runs in a

straight line, or with slight curvature to or near the base of the bill, and then bends abruptly downward at varying angles. The cutting edge of the upper mandible forms a re-entrance; lower, a corresponding salience. This character separates the group pretty sharply from other *Oscines*, excepting the *Icteridæ*.

All the species of the United States may be provisionally separated into four subfamilies, the European house sparrow constituting a fifth. These are the following: *Coccothraustinæ*, *Pyrgitinæ*, *Spizellinæ*, *Passerellinæ*, and *Spizinæ*.

Subfamily PYRGITINÆ.

This group is characterized by the following particulars: bill robust, turgid, and arched superiorly, but without distinct ridge. The lower mandible, at the basal part, is narrower than the upper. The nostrils are covered, and the side of the maxilla furnished with appressed bristles. The tarsi are short, and never exceed the middle toe in length. The tail is shorter than the slightly pointed wings.

In some respects, the *Pyrgitinæ* are similar to the *Coccothraustinæ*. In the short tarsi and covered nostrils, shorter and more rounded wings, and in the presence of stiff bristles upon the sides of the bill, they resemble this group. But the weaker feet, larger and more vaulted bill, and covered nostrils, are characters which distinguish them from the *Spizellinæ*.

Genus PYRGITA, Cuvier.

Gen. Char. Bill robust, turgid, and devoid of distinct ridge; superior and inferior outlines curved; margins inflexed; palate vaulted and without knob; nostrils concealed by sparse, short, incumbent feathers; sides of bill provided with stiff, appressed bristles. Tarsi short and stout, and never exceeding middle toes; claws short, stout, and much curved. Wings somewhat pointed, and longer than the tail, which is nearly even, emarginated, and but moderately rounded.

Pyrgita domestica, Cuv. The House Sparrow.

Sp. Char. Male: Upper parts chestnut-brown; summit of caput and nape, lower back, rump and tail coverts cinereous; interscapular feathers, on inner webs, streaked with black; chin, throat, lores, and narrow frontal line black; residue of inferior parts grayish, passing into white along the middle region. Behind the eye, running into the chestnut of the back, is a broad concolorous band; cheeks and lateral walls of neck white. Exterior of closed wings chestnut-brown, with the middle coverts marked with a broad white band; lesser coverts dark chestnut. Tail dark brown, bordered with pale chestnut. Mandibles black; feet reddish; iris brown.

Female: Duller colored and wanting the black of throat and face. Cheek cinereous; the eyes marked above and posteriorly by a yellow-ochre band. A similar colored band crosses the wings. Head and neck above ashy, tinged with brown; body superiorly, reddish cinereous, with longitudinal black streaks; breast and abdomen reddish-ash.

Length, 6.00; wing, 2.84; tail, 2.50; tarsus, .70; middle toe and claw, .60.

CHAPTER I.

THE SPARROW IN EUROPE.

This bird is quite common over the whole of the United Kingdom, including the islands of Orkney and Shetland. It is also found in Sweden, Norway, and Denmark; thence extending southward through Prussia, France, Spain, and Portugal, to Northern Africa, and eastward to Italy and Dalmatia. It is mostly restricted to the European Continent and the adjoining islands, although specimens have been obtained from Trebizond, the Nubian Mountains, the Himalaya Mountains, and other parts of India. Since the colonization of Australia by the English, these birds have been introduced, and are increasing rapidly in numbers, to the great detriment of native species.

This noisy, familiar, impatient bird is one of those creatures that manifest a close attachment to man, and follows him wherever he goes. Nothing seems to daunt his spirit. In the midst of the crowded and tumultuous city, among the queer sights and noises of the railroad station, and in the more retired and peaceful shades of the country farm, he is equally at home. He treats with the same indifference the slow-paced wagon, the rattling omnibuses and cabs, and the snorting engines.

Few species are more wary. Various devices in the form of traps, etc., are often used to capture these birds, but without much success. But at nights, when they have repaired to their roosting-quarters in hay-stacks and the common ivy, immense numbers are taken by means of nets and bags suspended from long poles. From their bold and obtrusive character, combined with their exceedingly ravenous appetite, we should naturally expect that these birds would become a ready prey to the snares of the fowler. Perhaps, their remarkable wariness may, in a measure, be attributed to the wholesale persecutions which they have met with at the hands of man during the past.

Bewick, in his History of British Birds, in describing the habits of this species, says, "It does not, like other birds, shelter itself in woods and forests, or seek its subsistence in uninhabited places, but is a resident in towns and villages; it follows society and lives at its expense; granaries, barns, courtyards, pigeon-houses, and, in short, all places where grain is scattered, are its favorite resorts."

According to the Count de Buffon "it is extremely destructive, its plumage is entirely useless, its flesh indifferent food, its notes grating to the ear, and its familiarity and petulance disgusting."

Mudie says the sparrows are "voracious, and withal energetic birds," and "may be seen holding assemblies with a deal of noise and clatter." Usually a dispute or quarrel seems to be the cause of these gatherings. In these troubles, the crowd which has been attracted invariably assists the strongest party. White, in his History of Selborne, briefly alludes to these convocations, and arrives at somewhat similar conclusions.

Yarrell contributes his testimony to the sparrow's pugnacity. After alluding to the early mating of this species, he says, "Like most of those birds which are very prolific, great animosity and numerous contests for choice or possession occur at this season of the year." In these battles, it is said by the above writer, "five or six individuals may be seen indiscriminately engaged, attacking, buffeting, and biting each other with all the clamor and fury of excited rage." These contests, after continuing for a longer or shorter period of time, are eventually concluded on an amicable basis, the respective combatants retiring from the struggle to attend to the more essential business of the season.

From the foregoing evidence, it is obvious that much of the character which the sparrow now possesses, was brought with it from its trans-Atlantic home. That this bird is jealous of strangers in its own native clime, and behaves with an insolent bearing towards them, and even bullies its own kindred when actuated by amatory influences, is too palpable to be doubted, or gainsaid. James Kirk, Esq., of Germantown, who emigrated to this country several years ago, has repeatedly called my attention to the irritable nature and pugnacious disposition of these birds, and remarked how alike is their behavior in America as compared with it in England. Others, no less competent to institute comparisons, have iterated and reiterated similar experiences.

The general movements of this species are characterized by marked vigilance, and a notable degree of energy and vivacity. When feeding, these birds are always on the alert, and are seldom, if ever, taken by surprise. They are mainly terrestrial, often repairing to trees for the purpose of resting and feeding.

Its flight is moderately firm, tolerably rapid, never very high, and but slightly protracted. In the fall these birds become gregarious, and move in varying flocks to their feeding-grounds, at more than the usual elevation.

The song of this species is too monotonous and shrill to afford gratification. Its position, as a member of the great Oscine group of *Aves*, has doubtless been given, not from any special development of musical ability, but from the presence of a singing apparatus. According to Macgillivray, its ordinary call is expressed by the dissyllabic word *phillip* or *yellop*.

Although its ordinary food consists of grain and insects, which are mainly procurable in the open country, yet it readily accommodates itself to a town life, and derives a subsistence from the refuse that is thrown out of houses. Its appetite is so accommodating that there is hardly any article of human diet which this bird will refuse. Fragments of potatoes, the refuse of a greengrocer's shop, a dry crust of bread, and a discarded bone, are equally attractive. "The market-places," according to Rev. J. G. Wood, "especially in those where vegetables are sold, as Covent Garden and Farringdon Market, the sparrow appears in great force, and in no way daunted by the multitudes of busy human beings that traverse the locality, flutters about their very feet, and feeds away without displaying the least alarm."

"In the Zoölogical Gardens, and in all large avaries," says the same distinguished writer, "the sparrow is quite in its element, pushing its way through the meshes of the wire roofs and fronts, pecking at the food supplied to the birds within, and retreating through the wires if attacked by the rightful owners of the plundered food. Even the majestic eagle is not free from the depredations of the sparrow, who hops through the bars of the cage with great impudence, feeds quite at his leisure on the scraps of meat that are left by the royal bird, and, within a yard of the terrible beak and claws, splashes about merrily in the eagle's bath. The large animals are also favored by constant visits from the sparrows, which hop about the rhinoceros, the elephant, the hippopotamus, or the wild swine, with utter indifference, skipping about close to their feet, and picking up grain as if they were the owners of the whole establishment."

In rural districts the sparrow subsists almost entirely upon insects and grains, the former constituting a large portion of its diet in the spring and early summer; and the latter, during the autumnal and winter months. As these birds congregate in immense flocks, and are exceedingly abundant, considerable quantities of grain are devoured. Consequently, they are much persecuted by the farmer, and their ranks continually decimated by guns, traps, nets, and other devices. Their services are so immense in the destruction of insects as to render them eminently useful to the agriculturist. A single pair of these birds has been known to carry to its young no less than forty grubs per hour, making an aggregate of about three thousand for the week. In every instance where the sparrows have been exterminated, there has been noticeable a proportional decrease in the crops from the depredations of insects. At Maine, for example, an entire destruction of these birds was authorized by law, and the result was that during the following year even the green trees were killed by caterpillars. A similar edict was proclaimed by the government at Auxerre, and like results followed.

In the fall, in addition to grain, various seeds, such

as the sow-thistle, groundsel, and the dandelion, which are classed among useless weeds, are eaten with avidity. The common white butterfly, whose larvæ are so noxious to the cabbage and other garden plants, is chased and killed in vast numbers. While feeding, these birds delight in company, and bands of variable numbers may be observed "all fluttering, and chirping, and pecking, and scolding, and occasionally fighting with amusing pertness."

A little incident of Mr. Wood's boyhood days is deserving of mention. So closely do these birds cluster, that the latter, when a boy, often amused himself by shooting them with sixpenny toy cannons, after attracting them to a small heap of oats which he had purposely thrown upon the stable floor; by thrusting the muzzles of his miniature guns through holes bored into the door, he was able to accomplish a due amount of destruction.

That the sparrow, even in Europe, is destructive to crops, is proved by the concurrent testimony of numerous writers. Mr. William Thompson, the author of "The Natural History of Ireland," says, in volume I. of that work,—

"In our garden, these birds were for a number of years very destructive to young peas, almost living upon and amongst them, perching on the pea-rod, and with their strong bills breaking through the pods to get at the peas, which they ate just when in perfection for the table.

"The proprietor of the nearest fields of grain to Belfast, in one direction (about a mile distant), complains loudly against hosts of town sparrows attacking his ripening crops. They go there early in the morning, and after satisfying their appetites at his expense, return to spend the day in town."

Selby, in the first volume of his work on British Ornithology, cites that it is reckoned by Low among the feathered denizens of the northern islands of Scotland, where it greatly annoys the agriculturist in the serious depredations which it commits upon bigg, a coarse variety of barley, the only grain that is grown to any extent in those remote settlements.

Mudie affirms that they commit some mischief upon small seeds when sown, upon patches of grain when first ripe, in the vicinity of villages and towns, and also, at certain seasons, upon the buds of shrubs and trees.

Yarrell says, "When summer advances, and the young birds of the year are able to follow the old ones, they become gregarious, flying in flocks together to the nearest field of wheat, as soon as the corn is sufficiently hardened to enable them to pick it out, and here for a time they are in good quarters; but when the corn is housed, and their supply cut off, they seek the adventitious meal which human habitations afford."

Sonini, in Dictionnaire d'Histoire Naturelle, published in 1817, says, "Sparrows are impudent parasites, living only in society with man, and dividing with him his grain, his fruit, and his home; they attack the first fruit that ripens, the grain as it approaches maturity, and even that which has been stored in granaries. Some writers have wrongly supposed that the insects destroyed by them compensated for their ravages on grain; eighty-two grains of wheat were crowded in the craw of a sparrow that had been shot by the writer, and Rougier de la Bergerie, to whom we owe excellent memoirs on rural economy, estimates that the sparrows of France consume annually ten million bushels of wheat."

Jardine says that a price is set on their heads on account of the depredations which they commit upon grains and garden seeds.

Valmont de Bomare, in his Dictionary, published in 1791, says, "In Brandebourg, in order to diminish the ravages committed by sparrows, a price is set on their heads, and the peasants are compelled by law to bring in a certain number yearly; in each village there are sparrow-hunters, who sell their birds to the peasants, to enable them to pay their tribute. The bird is bold, cunning, and quick in discerning snares or devices to frighten them; it breeds three times a year, feeding its young with insects, and especially bees, though its principal food consists of grain. It follows the farmer while sowing, harvesting, threshing, or in feeding his poultry; it enters the dovecot, and with its bill pierces the throats of young pigeons to obtain the grain in their craw."

That the sparrow's destructive propensities are well known in England, is attested to by Cowper's lines:—

> "The sparrows peep, and quit the sheltering eaves
> To seize the fair occasion; well they eye
> The scattered grain, and thievishly resolved
> To escape the impending famine, often scared,
> As oft return, a pert, voracious bird."

The following remarks, which are reproduced from the Bulletin of the French Acclimatization Society, concerning the "ravages committed by the Sparrows in Algeria," are taken from "The American Cultivator" for August 25, 1877. The writer says, "Wherever there are woods or plantations of trees, there the sparrows assemble in incredible numbers. One writer goes so far as to deplore the introduction of gum-trees, because they harbor the sparrows, and it is difficult to dislodge their nests from these slender, lofty trees.

"It is stated that on one estate alone, 200 acres of rye were so completely devoured by the sparrows before it was ripe, that not a single corn was harvested; and it was calculated that in a neighboring wood, some 150 acres in extent, there were 284,000 nests. One colonist complained that the sparrows had carried away two tons of his hay; and from the average weight of the nests weighed, it was estimated that ten tons of hay were carried away to construct these 284,000 nests. Further, it is stated that this same wood, which consists mainly of the Aleppo pine, is annually infested with caterpillars to such an extent that it is dangerous to go through it in the months of March and April, because the pine caterpillar is venomous. It seems that the sparrow, in Algeria at least, prefers grain to insect food."

A few thoughts from the pen of Mr. Knapp, in Cassell's Popular Natural History, conduct to the same inference. After expatiating briefly upon the friendly and sociable disposition of these birds among themselves, and their peculiar love for human society, he says, "The sparrow feeds on his (man's) food, rice, potatoes, and almost any other extraneous substance he may find in the street; looks to him for his support, and is maintained almost entirely by the industry and providence of man."

He who has been a constant reader of Nature, an English weekly devoted to science, for several years past, cannot have escaped the conclusion that the sparrow is destructive to blossoms. Thomas Cornber, of Newton le

Willows, England, in the issue of the above journal for May 10, 1877, substantially states that the sparrows do not attack the crocuses grown in his garden, but in that of a friend, living some miles away, their attacks are exclusively confined to the yellow ones, the purple variety escaping. He accounts for this preference on the supposition that the purple flowers possess some acrid or bitter property which renders them nauseous.

W. Von Freeden, of Hamburg, editor of the Hansa, in a communication to Nature for May 17, 1877, which is translated, says, "I have observed here that sparrows have shown a very considerable partiality for crocuses during this spring. My neighbor and I vied with each other in our spring beds; he excelled in yellow crocuses and hyacinths, I in white and blue crocuses. One beautiful Sunday the whole of his crocuses were found bitten and torn by sparrows, and what is noteworthy, also some yellow crocuses which had somehow wandered into my lot, while the blue and white remained untouched." Should this be regarded as an oversight, or was it a matter of taste? To offer a satisfactory explanation to this peculiar predilection of the sparrow, may not be classed among the impossibilities. Perhaps a dry spring, the color sense of the species, or even a more or less delicate mixture of the plant-sap, may account for it.

Corroborative of the last writer's observations appears in the issue of the same journal, dated May 31, the same year, a communication from an anonymous writer. He says, "I have for many years been a cultivator of the crocus, yellow, white, and purple; this spring they flowered abundantly, the white and purple blooming undisturbed, the yellow picked and torn."

Another individual, writing from Gray's Inn, attests to the foregoing assertions, but attributes these onslaughts to the town bird. The London bloom is specially attractive to the London sparrow, while in gardens remote from London, and surrounding it, plenty of yellow crocuses bloom, and are undisturbed. According to another writer, the leaves of the bird-cherry are eagerly attacked by the caterpillar of the pale-spotted ermine moth, during certain summers, to such an extent that the trees become ugly and stripped of their foliage by the middle, or end of July. Although the appetite of the sparrow can accommodate itself to nearly all kinds of food, yet it cannot be denied that it is, betimes, quite capricious. In autumn, the Guelder-rose, which adorns the English thicket with its beautiful red berries, presents an attractive and tempting sight, but birds seem to care very little for such fruit. Evidence, quite cumulative in its character, could be adduced to sustain the preceding statements, but enough has been given to prove the sparrow's destructive propensities. The bulk of testimony bearing upon this matter, which has appeared in Nature for many years past, points the same way.

If these birds are not destructive in a high degree, why begrudge them the grain which they pilfer? Why should the English peasant lad be employed, at a mere pittance, from early morning until the sun has gone down, armed with his clappers, to frighten away these greedy pilferers from the ruddy grain? Even before the days of "Little Boy Blue," of famous memory, down to the present time, have the same watchfulness and care been bestowed upon the fields of ripened grain, to guard them against their attacks.

Notwithstanding the injuries which are perpetrated upon crops and blossoms, which scarcely a writer will deny, does the good which these birds accomplish in the destruction of injurious insects amply compensate for the losses sustained? Let us see what evidence can be produced in justification of the sparrow.

Bewick remarks, as early as 1805, "In the destruction of caterpillars they are eminently serviceable to vegetation, and in this respect alone, there is reason to suppose, sufficiently repay the destruction they may make in the produce of the garden or the field."

Selby, who writes in 1833, says, "This bird feeds upon all kinds of grain and seeds, and, in the summer, destroys vast numbers of larvæ, moths, and butterflies, with which its young are principally fed; thus making ample compensation for the havoc it commits in the ripening fields of corn."

Mudie, in 1834, after briefly alluding to the destructive habits of the sparrow, affirms, "Upon the whole, they do much more good by the numbers of insects and caterpillars which they destroy. It is the house fly, as well as the thatch, and the eaves and holes in the roof, that bring them so much about dwellings; and in the consumption of these, as well as of crumbs and other refuse, they are most notable and indefatigable scavengers. But for them, the house flies would, in some situations, multiply to such an extent as to be intolerable; and were they not so incessant in their destruction of those prolific pests, the cabbage butterflies, it is doubtful whether one plant of the tribe could be reared in the market gardens."

The same writer asserts that, in France, in 1841, in the fine district of Burgundy, situated south of Auxerre, so much damage was done to crops from the extraordinary increase of caterpillars, resulting from the consequent destruction of small birds, that a law was passed prohibiting any further sacrifice of these creatures.

Macgillivray, in his History of British Birds, both Indigenous and Migratory, which was published in 1837, after referring to its devastation upon wheat, which is very perceptible in localities not remote from towns, as evidenced by the numerous earless stalks which are noticeable, and its fondness for the seeds of *Sinapis arvensis*, charlock, *Raphanus Raphanistum*, chickweeds and mouse ears, *Stellaria Cerastium*, and field and garden peas, says, "In summer it subsists partly on insects of various kinds, which also afford the chief nourishment of its young."

Yarrell, writing in 1843, says, "The young are fed for a time with soft fruits, young vegetables, and insects, particularly caterpillars, and so great is the number of these that are consumed by the parent birds, and their successive broods of young, that it is a question whether the benefit thus performed is not a fair equivalent for the grain and seeds required at other seasons of the year."

William Thompson, Esq., bears testimony in his Natural History of Ireland, which was published in 1849, to the good which these birds accomplish in the destruction of the large white garden butterfly (*Pontia brassica*), whose caterpillars are so injurious.

Dr. Brewer, in Forest and Stream, for June, 1877, says, "Ever since the commission, appointed by Louis Napoleon, at the head of which was that eminent *savan*, Florent Prevost, reported that the sparrow was *par eminence* the most useful to agriculture of all the birds of Europe, the sparrow has been protected by law, and the children in all the public schools of France, by order of the Department of Public Instruction, are taught the value of all birds, the sparrow not excepted." The doctor's authority for the above statement is the Hon. M. Servaux, who is head director of that department.

Other authorities could be quoted to show the good and evil results which are produced by the sparrow in its native country, but the writer is obliged to refer his readers to the bibliography of the subject which will be appended to this monograph. That immense good is accomplished in Europe by the services of these birds, must be admitted, if the testimonies adduced are worth anything. But it is greatly to be desired that a more complete inventory of the insects destroyed, than any hitherto published, should be given to the world. The mere assertion of the fact, which is all that we have to rely upon, in many instances, amounts to little in the writer's estimation. No work, with a single exception, has treated this subject as it deserves.

The sparrow is not one of the earliest risers among birds, but is certainly as wakeful as any of them. It begins to chatter with the dawn, and keeps up an animated conversation for an hour before forsaking its roost. Even before retiring for the night, its disagreeable chatter is heard to the annoyance of its human neighbors, for a similar period of time. As early as ten minutes before three o'clock in the morning this noise has been heard.

The nest of the sparrow is a very inartificial structure. It is composed of straw, hay, leaves, and other similar materials, externally; and is lined with a profusion of feathers. Although an exceedingly hardy bird, caring little for snow or frost, yet, nevertheless, it likes a warm bed to which it can retire when the arduous labors of the day are past. For this purpose, its resting place is crammed with feathers, which it procures from divers sources. Even their roosting quarters are similarly furnished. In the selection of a locality, these birds are by no means particular. Their nests have been discovered under the eaves of tiles, in creviced walls, in decayed trees, and even in the orifices of old water-pipes; in short, wherever the necessary materials can be accumulated. Walls overgrown with ivy are favorite places of resort, both for building and roosting purposes. The immense numbers of nests which are built under the nests of the larger birds in a rookery can only be imagined by those who have witnessed such places.

Sometimes, but rarely, these birds take to trees. The higher branches of the apple and plum are ordinarily chosen, but, when any other tree is selected, which is occasionally done, it is never situated very far from an occupied human dwelling. In such situations, the structure is invariably domed, and is provided with an entrance in the side. Externally, it is composed of a profusion of hay; and is lined with a dense mass of feathers. It is a large and rather clumsy affair.

Not unlike other familiar birds, the sparrow is somewhat capricious in its choice of locality. Several examples are upon record of nests being placed on different parts of a ship's rigging. For example, while the Great Britain was lying in the Sandom graving-dock, two nests were constructed by certain sparrows in the "bunts" of the main and mizzen topsails. Mr. Thompson cites the case of a nest which was placed upon the furled sail of the Aurora, of Belfast. This nest, which remained intact during the first voyage of that vessel to Glasgow, was loosened during the second trip, and both it and the eggs which it contained, were destroyed. Again, a pair of sparrows nidificated underneath the slings of the foreyard of the ship Ann of Shields, just preparatory to leaving port. When the vessel reached its destined port upon the Tyne, the birds went ashore, and shortly returned with materials with which to finish their homes.

The chief external ornament of the Rotunda, in Dublin, is a superbly carved frieze. It represents the heads of oxen, and is beautifully festooned with flowers, which are pendant from the horns. The frieze encircles the entire building at a considerable elevation. In the hollow of the eye of one of these heads, a sparrow placed its nest. Among other materials which the bird had utilized for this purpose, was a woollen thread with a noose at one extremity ; by some strange accident, wholly inexplicable, the little creature got the noose around his neck, and in his desperate exertions to release himself from the unhappy situation, dropped from his nest, and hung suspended below. The most prodigious efforts were made to escape the threatened death, but in vain. Unhappily his remains were gibbeted at his own door, and were to be seen swaying to and fro in the gentlest breeze, while the straws of his nest protruded from the eye-hole right over his head.

Mr. Thompson asserts that, in country places, this species usually places its nests in spouts, and thus stops the course of the rain, causing the house to be overflowed. When ejected from such places, it is said to resort to the branches of the balm of Gilead and the spruce, which it prefers to deciduous trees. According to the same authority, it often builds in rookeries; occasionally takes possession of the nest of the house martin, which is generally tenantless at the time, and as frequently usurps the burrow of the sand martin, before the vernal return of this species to the home of its nativity.

Mr. Gould, in writing about this bold and fearless little creature, confirms much of what the previous writer has expressed.

He says, "It is not a little annoying to watch closely the ways and doings of our constant attendant, the sparrow, who, as if presuming upon our friendship, sets no bounds to his impudence towards his feathered brethren, and with great effrontery, frequently seizes upon the hole selected by the starling when absent from its nest, and continues to hold possession until the starling, losing all patience, takes him by the neck, and with main force draws him from the hole. This little altercation ended, and the stronger bird in possession, matters grow more amicable. It not unfrequently happens that the fairy martin, which constructs her nest under the eaves of our houses, has scarcely finished her labors ere the sparrow seizes on the building. The martin is said to revenge itself upon the intruder in a curious way. To fight so powerful a bird would answer no end, she therefore plasters up the entrance to the nest with mud, and keeps him a prisoner."

The sparrow is quite prolific, and raises several broods in a single season. It has been known to rear no less than fourteen young during that period. It is a very affectionate parent, and is not uncommonly observed in the midst of crowded streets feeding its young, which, while sitting upon the ground, manifest their hungry eagerness, by the manner in which they open their bills and flap their wings.

The eggs of this species are usually five in number,

although six sometimes constitutes a nest full. They are grayish-white in ground-color, and profusely covered with spots and dashes of gray-brown. They vary, however, in markings, and it is quite common to find in the same nest eggs that are nearly black with the mottlings, and others with few if any spots or stripes at all.

The young, according to Macgillivray, in progressing towards maturity, pass through the following stages: "At first moult, completed by beginning of winter, males assume colors of adult birds, although it is not until next season that they are perfected; females also acquire deeper tints. In the second plumage the male is as follows: Upper mandible light grayish-brown, lower flesh colored with tip brown; feet pale brown, upper part of head brownish-gray; preocular space blackish-gray; line over the eye extending down neck, yellowish-gray mixed with chestnut-brown; some lateral feathers of neck little chestnut near tip; auricular coverts greenish-gray; forepart of neck, breast, abdomen, light yellowish-gray, fading posteriorly into white; a broad band down foreneck from mandible obscurely black, that color being concealed by whitish tips of feathers. Anterior dorsal and scapular feathers light yellowish-brown, their inner web brownish-black at tip; posterior dorsal and upper tail coverts light greenish-gray; lower tail coverts light yellowish-gray. Tail wood-brown, margined with gray; smaller wing coverts light brown, with little chestnut near tips; quills dusky externally, margined with yellowish-brown; primary coverts the same; secondary coverts with a broader external margin of yellowish-brown; the first row of small coverts tipped with paler yellowish-brown.

As the bird becomes older, its colors assume a richer tint, until the wings and back become bright chestnut, and bar in former is pure white."

In view of the astonishing increase of this species in Europe, are there no checks thereto, in the shape of natural enemies? The last-mentioned writer, in his history of this bird, says in England they are preyed upon by the merlin, sparrow hawk, and weasel, and perhaps by other quadrupeds, as well as by boys, cockney sportsmen, and field naturalists. The mode of capture employed by boys is thus described. For this purpose a trap is constructed in this wise: two bricks are placed parallel to each other, while a third is laid across one of their extremities; another brick, or a piece of board or slab, is placed between the parallel bricks, and supported by the aid of a vertical stick, the lower extremity of which reposes upon the edge of a brick arranged transversely. The trap being prepared, is then baited with oatmeal, bread, or other edible substances. In attempting to get the bread, the prop becomes removed, the lid falls, and the sparrow remains a prisoner.

Immense numbers are also captured at night, while perching among the ivy, their favorite roosting quarter, by means of a net manufactured for that express purpose.

CHAPTER II.

THE SPARROW IN AMERICA.

This species, which was introduced into several portions of our country a few years ago, has increased so rapidly in numbers that it is now accounted one of our most familiar denizens. Before another decade has passed, unless measures are taken to check its wonderful diffusion, the result of its rapid propagation, it will be safe to predict a general overflow of the entire country.

The earliest attempt to introduce these birds was apparently made in the autumn of 1858, by Deblois, in Portland, Maine. To the number of six they were let loose in a large garden near the centre of the city. The following winter was spent in the immediate locality, shelter from the inclement weather being obtained underneath the porch of a neighboring church. In the spring of 1859 three nests were built, in only one of which the parents were successful in rearing a family. Two broods consisting of ten young birds resulted from this union. The birds continued to multiply, and ultimately became so numerous, that as early as the winter of 1871 they reached the town of Rockland of the same State.

In 1860 Eugene Schieffelin, of New York, imported twelve of these birds, and set them at liberty in the vicinity of Madison Square in that city. Several years in succession the experiment was repeated. In 1864 fourteen birds were released in Central Park by the Commissioners. Others were subsequently brought from England by different individuals, and set free at Jersey City. The latter have since multiplied so rapidly that their offspring have spread to adjoining towns, and are now social residents in all the large cities and towns around New York, as well as in every portion of that great metropolis itself.

It was not, however, until 1868 that the sparrow was introduced into Boston. Two hundred birds were then purchased in Germany, by the city government, but only about twenty reached their destination. These were released in the month of June, but, unfortunately, several died from disease, or from weakness induced by sea-voyage; the remnant disappeared. In the ensuing summer others were brought over, only ten of which survived. The survivors were carefully housed and nourished, and only restored to freedom when in excellent condition. Released from confinement, they quickly flew away, and nothing was seen of them for several months, when, unhappily, they turned up in the southern part of the city, whither they had betaken themselves. In the immediate vicinity of stables, for which they apparently manifested a preference, they built their houses and reared their families. There they remained until the approach of winter, when they returned to the city to the number of one hundred and fifty, where they were regularly fed by the city-forester each day in the Deer Park. At night they roosted in the thatched roofs of the buildings.

Near the close of the winter of 1869 these birds were brought to Philadelphia. To John Bardsley, Esq., of Germantown, belongs the credit of their introduction.

For many years our lawn and shade trees had been infested by measuring worms, much to the annoyance of pedestrians. Nothing could be done to remedy the matter. The nuisance became yearly worse and worse. The good effects of the sparrows, in other cities, in ridding the squares and parks of insect-pests, were too well known through the public papers to allow of much hesitation upon the part of the people. Councils were petitioned for relief. For many long months the question was agitated, but seemingly with little hope of a speedy settlement. At this crisis Mr. Bardsley was projecting a visit to his native land. Sympathizing with his city brethren, preparatory to starting upon his journey he sought an interview with leading councilmen in relation to bringing over a goodly number of birds on his return. Nothing satisfactory was elicited. Having completed his arrangements, Mr. Bardsley sailed for England, determining, should he reach home, to collect a thousand or two of birds at his own expense, and present them to the city of his adoption. In due season he reached Ashton, his native town, and had actually commenced work when he received the startling yet doubtless joyful intelligence that the sparrow difficulty had been settled by Councils, and he was the city's authorized agent. With his characteristic zeal and energy Mr. Bardsley applied himself vigorously to the task, and, with the assistance of several lads, succeeded in obtaining, in the course of a few days, more than a thousand birds. Having secured his cargo, and everything being in readiness, he sailed from Liverpool, and after many trials and a few vicissitudes of fortune, reached Philadelphia early in March. His numerous and troublesome charges were at once surrendered to the authorities. Owing to the inclemency of the season they were comfortably quartered, and provided with every needful attention. In the latter part of April, the weather becoming mild, they were released from their long confinement, to fly whither they chose. In the best of condition, the result of the attention and care bestowed upon them since their arrival, and emancipated at a period when nature was buoyant with life, and all aglow with beauty and song, there could be no obstacle to their easy acclimatization, and consequent multiplication and diffusion.

Later, these birds were introduced into Utah, in the vicinity of Great Salt Lake, where they have become quite common; and still later in Indianapolis, Ia., where they have grown to be so troublesome that the inhabitants would gladly get rid of them at almost any cost. An effort is now being made to introduce them into North Carolina, under the fancied belief that they will prove highly beneficial in the destruction of noxious insects, but I hope that it will not succeed. The agent for their introduction has lately become convinced of their utter worthlessness, and has so informed his friends.

Few species of birds display less suspicion, greater caution, and more pugnacity, than the subject of our sketch. It delights to dwell in close proximity to human dwellings, and apparently affects a fondness for man's society. While thus manifesting considerable confidence in man, as shown by its familiar manners, it, however, possesses so many unenviable traits as not to merit the full measure of his esteem and approbation. The insolence of its deportment, sneaking, thievish propensities, and above all, its pugnacity, rapacity, and destructiveness, render it an object of profound contempt.

Its pugnacity, the certain outgrowth of an extremely jealous and irritable nature, manifests itself in various ways. By a limited few, it is alleged that this feeling is confined to the males, and only exhibited among themselves when actuated by amatory influences. This is a gross mistake. It is manifested at all times, and is as conspicuous among the females as among their more powerful lords. It is chiefly during the breeding-period that these contentions occur among themselves. Territorial possession is the *casus belli*. Males and females mingle promiscuously, and it is quite difficult to determine which of the sexes displays the greater valor. The struggle frequently commences between a pair of males, and assumes gigantic proportions. The females at first stand aloof, maintain almost perfect silence, and only enter the arena when the conflict seems utterly hopeless on one side or the other. The loud clamors and menacing gestures of the belligerents soon attract their feathered brethren, who enter the lists, and at once take part with one or the other of the contending factions. These struggles often continue for nearly a half hour unless stopped by human interference, and break up as quickly and as mysteriously as they are precipitated. A careful study of the manœuvres of the opposing parties have convinced me that a very close kinship subsists among the individuals of each side.

These quarrels occur less frequently, however, during the feeding process, and are not restricted to any particular season. When there is a rich supply of appropriate food-stuffs hundreds of birds may be seen feeding together, and the utmost harmony and good-will be observable. But let there be a paucity of regimen, and the birds are not slow to perceive the fact, the spirit of

greed is soon in the ascendant, and a quarrel ensues.
The same unhappy condition of affairs occurs when a
pair of birds or a family group has most fortunately
come across an article of luxury, and is disturbed by the
approach of strangers who endeavor to wrest from them
the much coveted booty.

But it is not so much on account of these family difficulties that our repugnance to the sparrow arises. Do
not our native species, in many instances, have their
domestic infelicities, less bitter and less lasting though
they be? It is mainly owing to its domineering and
insolent bearing towards the latter that we detest the
sparrow. Who has not witnessed frequent manifestations of the hostile conduct of this foreigner? In the
spring, when our migrants return from their winter
homes to the scenes of conjugal bliss and domestic felicity, they are received by these strangers with the most
perfect coolness and stolid apathy. Should they venture to take up their quarters in places rendered sacred
and dear by the associations of the past, they are instantly
beset and driven away. Their former territory has been
taken possession of, and they must look elsewhere. A
near approach to accustomed haunts is sure to be found
out, and instant vengeance wreaked upon their temerity. These birds lay claims to occupied spots, and
prepare to defend them at all hazards. What individual
courage cannot accomplish is effected by stratagem, or
by combination. Many of our most useful birds are
objects of these unmerited assaults, and unable to cope
with prodigious numbers are compelled to forsake accustomed sites for less congenial places. The lawns and
groves which surround the residences of opulence, that
once rang with the merry notes of the robin and song

sparrow, now resound with the disagreeable noise of this sparrow.

The extraordinary salacity of these birds, which is almost as conspicuous a feature of their existence during cold weather as during the season of breeding, begets, beyond the shadow of a doubt, a feeling of jealousy which graduates into one of intense hatred towards other species should they venture within forbidden grounds, and even shows itself in a much lighter form towards their fellow-companions. As a consequence of this abnormal sexual condition, the desire to nidificate commences remarkably early, and continues rather late, often lasting from February to November.

Having dwelt upon the sparrow's treatment of other species, at considerable length, it becomes necessary to inquire whether our native birds do not occasionally manifest a little of the spirit of pugnacity towards the foreign invader. To do otherwise would seem unnatural. Birds, like their human brethren, become strongly attached to the homes of their nativity, and show a willingness and readiness to protect them against assault. Among many species there is apparent a friendly and neighborly feeling, which tolerates others within their territories. Instances of the existence of this noble trait are not wanting. The robin, song and chipping sparrow, have been known to fraternize with other species, and to live upon the most amicable terms with them. The same good and kindly feeling would be shown towards the sparrow, were there a disposition to reciprocate it. I have observed such a disposition upon the part of the song sparrow, and its very near relative, the hair bird, on scores of occasions, but there has always been manifest a want of inclination upon the part of the house sparrow to notice these friendly advances, or a tendency to repel them most unceremoniously and ungenerously.

Cruel as is the treatment which our smaller birds receive from the stranger, when they have returned, after a brief sojourn abroad, to the land of their birth, they bear it quite patiently and nobly, and only venture to resent the insults which are heaped upon them when forbearance ceases to be a virtue. To witness this usurpation of rightful territory and the insolent bearing of the marauder, is certainly very provoking, and to the robin, whose ideas of honor and right are very exalted, must be considered a just cause for war. It is not surprising then that this " bouncer of the sod" should wage persistent warfare upon the enemy, on each annual return, but to be ingloriously defeated. The bluebird, a very obstinate little fellow, to be sure, has learned from experience the folly of contending against superior numbers, and, consequently, leaves the sparrow in undisputed possession of subjugated territory. In past years I have seen this bird contend with the sparrow for the possession of a tree-cavity, or a box, with a courage which was truly commendable and astonishing, but to no use.

In not a single case have I known either the robin or the bluebird to come off victors in these encounters. In a single-handed struggle I would have but little fears for them. While this has been the experience of competent observers in other cities, also, there can be no doubt but that the sparrows are sometimes beaten and driven away, the conquerors remaining masters of the situation. The experience of Dr. Brewer, of Boston, confirms this suspicion. When told by Mr. Galvin, the city-forester of Boston, that the bluebird assails the sparrow, and expels it from its home, the doctor suddenly remembers that, in various instances, throughout his experience, the former is always the aggressor.

Mr. Galvin affirms substantially that our native birds have nothing to fear from the sparrow. Not the least animosity is manifested towards either the robin or the bluebird. The little chipping sparrow is its friend, and is often found feeding with it upon the same bit of bread. Bluebirds, which were wanting on the Common before the introduction of the sparrows, are now quite plentiful. The martins, attracted by the number of boxes, have wonderfully increased. These two species we are informed are the inveterate enemies of the sparrows, treating them badly, seizing their boxes, and breaking up their nests. These indignities, it is natural to be supposed, would be resented; but in the contest which is provoked, we are told that the bluebirds "are always too strong for them." Evidence is not wanting to show that the reverse of this is equally true. In the proper place the testimony both *pro* and *con* will be set forth.

The impudence of the sparrow has certainly not escaped notice. For boldness, this species of *avis* has no parallel. The crow is a paragon of excellence when brought into contrast. While the fowls are being fed, flocks of fifty, and even more, assemble in the poultry-yard, and wilfully defraud the occupants of their due allowances. When detected and driven away, I will not say frightened away, for they are strangers to fear, they repair to a short distance, alight upon any neighboring object, and, as if to show their utter disgust and indignation, break forth in a full chorus of loud and uncouth vociferations. With eyes intently fixed upon the much coveted fare, they bide their time, although rather impatiently, and when the disturber of their meal has turned his back and is out of sight, repair with all possible speed to the feeding ground, and there gorge themselves to satiety. All the while they are thus occupied, they do not permit themselves to be surprised; for, with half-averted look, the stealthiest approach is noticed, and the flock is off in the twinkling of an eye. In this respect, there is a manifest difference between this species and others which relax this general vigilance by appointing a few individuals to act as guards.

The chickens evidently do not entertain the highest feelings of regard for these *gamins*, as shown by the fierce attacks which they make upon them whenever they insinuate themselves into their presence. These assaults subserve but a temporary purpose, for the sparrows hop carelessly aside, or fly to a short distance when vigorously pressed, and subsequently resume their labors as though nothing had happened. Instances have occurred, in the writer's experience, of this boldness being carried to extremes. A case in point I will now proceed to mention.

In the summer of 1877 I raised several broods of chicks, which it was the custom to feed at six o'clock in the morning, and at the same time at the close of the day. While thus occupied, the sparrows, as if by a sort of intuition, would come in vast numbers, and very contentedly perch upon the adjoining trees, preparatory to making a meal of Indian corn. Their approach was quite silent, only a few coming together. Sometimes their presence was unknown and unobserved, so quietly did they deport themselves. But when the person, whose duty it was to attend to this business, would disappear from the scene, the ground would soon be covered by birds, some of which would enter the coops, taking due care, however, to avoid the bill of the enraged hen

Jealousy is certainly the *vera causa* of the sparrow's irritability and pugnacity. This feeling is so deeply ingrained into its very being that the slightest cause will evoke it. The presence of a stranger bird when the feeding process is going on, is enough to arouse suspicion and lead to trouble. Perhaps jealousy is the natural outgrowth of long-continued exertions for maintenance in the "struggle for existence." The wonderful salacity of this species, and its remarkable powers of reproduction, lend countenance to this belief. A species that breeds freely, and multiplies rapidly, must doubtless perish, where bounteous provisions for its subsistence are not made in the wise economy of nature. Particularly will this be found to be the case in regions in which the natural harmony of things is spoiled by man's shortsightedness and stupidity. Either nature must most miraculously increase her supply to satisfy the growing demand, or else a long and bitter struggle for supremacy will inevitably ensue, the weaker go to the wall, or be compelled to migrate to other quarters. Thus will be engendered a feeling of jealousy, if not of intense hatred, upon the part of the stronger against the weaker, which will manifest itself in bitter persecutions and lifelong quarrels. Just such a situation of things as I have depicted, must be patent to all who are not blinded by prejudice, if they will but use their powers aright.

In by-gone years, many of our smaller winter denizens were daily to be seen in our gardens and on our lawns. Who does not recollect the pleasure and joy which their presence afforded? The song sparrow, tree sparrow, and even the active little black-capped titmouse, would hop about the door, and, by their well-known calls, solicit, as it were, the refuse of the kitchen. Upon the summit of a bush or a tree, or perched upon the fence, they would patiently wait until the poultry had been fed and had retired, when they would gladly descend to the yard, and thankfully receive what their stronger brethren had left. But now the grounds are thoroughly policed by the sparrows, and our native birds compelled to keep at a wary distance, or only venture to peck a few grains during the temporary absence of their masters. During the prevalence of cold weather, the sparrows are a constant source of annoyance by their presence and noise, save when they retire to their roosting-quarters, at the close of the day. But with the rising sun, and, in some instances, long before his slanting rays are seen in the east, they are on hand, ready to seize, with their characteristic avidity, whatever comes in sight. The strictest vigilance is necessary to prevent their wanton pillages.

In the spring, save during the season of harvest and fruitage, their attentions are somewhat intermitted. The duties of nidification, incubation, and brood-raising demand a considerable share of attention. Hence their presence, except during the mornings and evenings, is notably scarce. While they take their breakfast and supper upon the writer's premises, their homes are elsewhere. The lack of suitable accommodations is mainly the cause of this seeming preference. A near neighbor having erected comfortable houses for them, we are thus saved much annoyance.

It is only during their absence, consequent upon the discharge of home duties, that a few of our native birds pay us a slight call, occasionally. It is during these visits, as if reluctant to desert entirely the scenes of past associations, that a few are seized with an irresistible desire to build. While some are most summarily frustrated in any such endeavor, others are not wanting that meet with a due degree of success. I cannot forbear to mention in this connection an incident which happened during the month of June, 1877. A pair of robins visited my lawn, emboldened by the absence of the enemy; and, being lured by the aspect of the scenery, they almost instantly set to work to build themselves a home. The summit of a tall and rather dense maple afforded a suitable and retired site. Their advent was unobserved. The almost perfect silence which they maintained whilst engaged in its construction was truly wonderful. Even the keen and vigilant gaze of the sparrow was eluded. The nesting-tree occupied the centre of a grass-plot, and stood but fifteen feet from my doorstep. Troops of noisy children whiled away their merry moments beneath its sheltering boughs, without so much as disturbing the busy workers, or catching a glimpse of their quite familiar forms. The chosen site was doubtless the inevitable result of mature reflection, for, at this point, a cherry tree blended its dark green foliage with that of the red maple. So thickly and intricately were the leaves and branches interlaced, that the most acute vision could not pierce the almost impenetrable network. Thus concealed, the nest would have remained unknown, had not a most curious circumstance revealed its presence. The robins could have entered the nest and retired therefrom as often as they chose without being perceived by human or feathered enemies, so artfully was it hidden, and so favorably situated was the tree. But this fancied security was destined to be of short continuance. My son, a lad of twelve years, was the first to call attention to its existence. The discovery was wholly accidental. In the exercise of his scansorial powers, a failing to which the generality of lads is prone, he unexpectedly fell upon the structure. At this time it contained but three eggs which were slightly altered. From some strange and mysterious cause, the sparrows, seemingly, had not observed this trespass upon their grounds, my son's discovery antedating theirs by a couple of days. On reflection, the circumstance does not seem so mysterious after all. To reach the poultry-yard unobserved by their human persecutors, they were compelled to make a circuitous journey; by so doing, they avoided altogether the tree which supported the robin's nest. These raids upon the poultry-yard were always made in the morning and evening. The robins were doubtless apprised of the fact, and shaped their actions accordingly. During the intervening time less caution was necessary, as the visits of the sparrows were quite infrequent.

The cherry tree had now begun to ripen its fruits. The sparrows were not slow in making the discovery. From the poultry-yard fence the tempting cherry could be easily seen as it dangled from its flexible stem. The keen eye of the robin discerned it in the near distance. The temptation was not to be resisted. They sallied out of their well-hidden retreat to taste the luscious fruit, but, alas! they were espied by the sparrows, who had already taken possession of the trees, in vast numbers. They were instantly assailed and driven from the neighborhood. Four times in succession they labored to regain possession, but without avail. Defeated and disheartened, they removed to more congenial quarters, leaving their home and its treasures to the cruel mercies of a relentless foe. On revisiting the nest two days subsequently, the eggs were gone. They had either been spirited away by the authors, or destroyed by the enemy.

A better example of the sparrow's pugnacity and vengeful spirit than the preceding, could certainly not be given. Were these its only faults we might charitably hide them from view, and extend to these extremely familiar creatures a most generous welcome. But their excessively rapacious and vigorous appetites lead them into wrong doings. Being omnivorous birds, they do not carefully discriminate between the cultivated varities of our fruits, and their wild, untamed prototypes; and between the seeds of gramineous plants growing wild, and our cultivated cereals. Their destructive propensities, though well attested, are not as fully appreciated by the popular mind as they should be. Agriculturists and small fruit growers will do well to master the details of their history, and accord to them the welcome which their merits, rather their demerits, amply deserve.

'Tis true this species has received most flattering encomiums from casual observers, but the writer certainly cannot bear the best of testimony to its usefulness. As it is not as destructive to noxious insects as many of our smaller native birds, its presence seems unnecessary. During the breeding-period, I admit, many caterpillars are destroyed and fed to the young, but even this good is more than outweighed by the mischief which is committed.

Its indubitable hatred of native species; the depredations which are perpetrated upon the tender buds of herbaceous plants, shrubs, and trees; the wholesale destruction of the blossoms of the apple, pear, and cherry, and the fruits of the same; the wanton devastations which are committed upon the vines when the grapes are mellowing, are powerful incentives for those who have suffered from their ravages to urge the authorities to colonize and send them back to England where the peasantry are paid for potting them into sparrow pies. They are always feeding, but unlike most species, grow corpulent upon what they pilfer, and thus set the unwholesome example of consuming what they do not earn.

The food of this species is both vegetal and animal in character, but chiefly the former. Latterly, fewer insects are destroyed than formerly. This is readily accounted for. Now, in many of our large towns and cities, these birds are so well fed and pampered that they are either too lazy to hunt caterpillars, or else the presence of better and more nutritious food has created in them a disgust, or rather disrelish, for insect-diet. In rural localities, the abundance of plant-life in divers forms constitutes a rich field for the display of their granivorous and frugivorous propensities.

It is ghastly rubbish to pretend, as a special few seem to do, that the ridding of our trees of caterpillars and hemiptera can be intrusted to the sparrows. Almost any bird, from an ostrich to a humming-bird, may or does eat, insects. This diet is not restricted to the technically designated insectivorous birds. In the general scheme of nature, insects and birds are natural complements, the one balancing the other. Sparrows certainly do not come under this category. They are a conirostral and granivorous species, and take to insect fare just as a hawk, a crow, a grakle, or any of our native finches.

During the cold weather these birds derive a rather precarious subsistence from the seeds of our commonest weeds and grasses. They assemble about our doors for the crumbs and scraps from the table. Throughout the different seasons, and in all places, hundreds of them may be seen upon our principal thoroughfares, scratching among the excrement of horses for whatever of nutrient qualities may be found therein.

Their winter fare consists of the seeds of *Chenopodium album*, *Amarantus hybridus*, *A. albus*, *A. paniculatus*, *Rumex sanguineus*, *Ambrosia artemisiæfolia*, and besides those of the different asters and solidagos.

When balmy spring has melted the icy fetters of winter, and started the sap through its accustomed channels, the sparrows, active and hardy creatures though they are, become endowed with new vigor, sally out from their winter retreats while plant life is budding into bloom, and wantonly destroy without stint or pity.

In the months of April and May, they enter our lawns and indiscriminately attack whatever of vegetation is coming into existence. The maples, particularly *Acer rubrum* and *A. Saccharinum*, are rifled of their blossoms. The kitchen-garden does not escape their visits. The cherry, and the various species of *Pyrus* and *Prunus*, are devastated for the ripened stamens and immature ovaries. Many of our herbaceous plants are bitten before they have attained to the height of a few inches above the ground. In the floral stage, primroses and others, are hopelessly ruined. The grape-vines are attacked, and the blossoms pillaged. Later, during the middle of June, when the cherry has ripened its fruit, the destruction is immense. Scarcely a tree escapes. The fruit is seldom eaten in its entirety, but bitten in several places, thus causing premature decay. Several trees that I examined, which were literally crowded with fruit, did not reveal a single untouched cherry One small branch, containing a hundred cherries, had every one bitten; some in a semi-rotten condition, in consequence. The so-called honey cherry has the greatest attraction, and the common black cherry the least, showing that the species is somewhat fastidious in its appetite, notwithstanding its decided penchant for horsedung. But is there no way of preventing this destruction? I apprehend not. The scarecrow is of little avail. Even the report of a gun creates but a momentary alarm; for the very next moment the birds are back, feeding as vigorously as before, as though nothing had happened. For man, creation's lord, they have but little fear or respect. I have known instances where they would enter a tree, alight within a few feet of a person, and feed away as though they were not cognizant of his presence, all the while keeping a wide lookout for dangers. The American sparrow is a fond lover of the juicy cherry, and destroys many when allowed to visit the trees unmolested. He is characterized by greater boldness than his European kin, who is desperately afraid of man, his inveterate persecutor. It had been hoped that the strawberry would have remained unmolested. But no; this most luscious berry must share a similar fate. During the past season, a friend of the writer's, living in Germantown, was surprised to find that the sparrows were at work upon his neighbor's strawberry patch. As soon as the fruit had turned, it was plucked and eaten upon the spot, or borne in triumph to the nest, a box upon the premises (a poor compensation for hospitality shown). To prevent these ravages the gentleman was compelled to cover the bed, which was a small one, with netting stretched upon small upright stakes.

The cultivated raspberry is also esteemed a great luxury. During the prevalence of the season, from the middle of June until about the middle of July, the sparrows are constant visitors to the bushes. The red variety is greatly to be preferred to any other. The black variety is the least attractive. It is probable that the fruits of the high and low blackberries are occasionally eaten, although not to any great extent. I have seen birds upon these bushes acting very mysteriously. A subsequent examination showed that the berries had been pecked. The pea-vines receive their share of attention also. But it is only when the pods have appeared and become partially swollen out with the developing peas. When the latter have attained one-fourth, and even one-half, their natural size, they are most prized. They are secured by the separation of the valves of the pod by the bill of the bird. The destruction which these birds commit upon the pea is nothing when compared with that which they perpetrate upon grain fields. The growing head is often attacked, and the soft and milky grain extracted from the glume. But it is mainly after the head has ripened, and is reposing upon the field preparatory to being carried to the barn for shelter, that this destruction is most complete. Many a grain is then pulled from its hiding-place and passed into the stomachs of these birds, or scattered irrecoverably upon the ground. In the summer of 1877 immense flocks of these birds, numbering from a hundred to five hundred, were observed two miles to the southwest of Chestnut Hill, a suburb of Philadelphia, in the midst of a large field of cradled grain. They were vigorously at work, and, contrary to what is usual, so intently bent upon their task as not to notice the writer and two friends, until we were within a few feet of them. Then, all of a sudden, they rose up, but to re-alight a few seconds afterwards, within fifty yards of their former place. To assert that these flocks would destroy and waste at least twenty-five bushels, in less than half a day, would not be beyond the range of possibility. Other fields were witnessed during the summer, undergoing similar depredations, on quite as extensive a scale; so that the mischief done during a single season, in a limited area, can hardly be estimated.

In addition to the above articles, the seeds of some cruciferous and compositaceous plants are also eaten. After the soil has been loosened in early spring, and sown, these birds assemble upon the newly raked ground, and in an incredibly short time gather up the scattered seeds, leaving but few to germinate. Those of the garden lettuce (*Lactuca sativa*), radish (*Raphanus sativus*), cabbage (*Brassica oleracea*), are principally desired. When these plants have matured their seeds, their dried heads and pods are visited. The seeds of the dandelion, and our common thistles, are torn from their receptacles, and devoured at the appropriate seasons.

During the autumnal months, when the grapes are beginning to mellow, these birds are on hand. In some localities the bunches are so horribly mutilated as to be of no use. They attack the grape in the same manner as they do the cherry. Few of our cultivated varieties escape. The small winter grape (*Vitis cordifolia*), on account of its peculiar flavor and small pulp, is never attacked, although I am inclined to believe that the sweet-scented blossoms are not so fortunate. The fruit of the sweet viburnum (*Viburnum lentago*), which is in excellent order in the months of October and November, is eaten with a gusto. The fruits of *Lonicera periclymenum* and *Rhus glabra* constitute a portion of their bill of fare also at this season, although not favorite articles of diet.

Many careful microscopic examinations of the contents of numerous stomachs during the fall and winter months, September excluded, have revealed but few, if any, traces of insects. It is therefore wise to conclude that their diet then consists almost entirely of vegetable food, using this term in its broadest sense. In early spring indubitable traces of *Harpalus pennsylvanicus*, *H. compar*, *Casnonia pennsylvanica*, and *Formica sanguinea*, in small quantities, have been found. From the small number of coleoptera and hymenoptera that I have been able to find, I incline to the opinion that this scarcity is to be attributed either to general dislike for such fare, or to its accidental presence. The examination of many stomachs, without the slightest trace of insect remains, seems to confirm the latter suspicion.

It is mainly during the breeding-period that the parent birds destroy vast number of noxious caterpillars, and others. The principal insects which constitute the dietary of the young then, are the larvæ of *Gortyna zeæ*, *Anisopteryx vernata*, *A. pometaria*, *Zerene catenaria*, *Ennomos subsignaria*, *Chærodes transversata*, *Hybernia tiliaria*, *Pieris rapæ*, *Colias philodice*, *Thecla humuli*, *Utethesia bella*, *Plusia precationis*, and *Orgyia leucostigma*, among lepidoptera. The larva of *Gortyna zeæ*, or the corn worm as it is commonly designated, is but little utilized as food, owing to the great difficulty experienced in its capture. During the prevalence of the cabbage plague a few years ago, vast numbers of *Pieris rapæ* were destroyed. The birds evidently did some good in the preservation of the plants. Last year but few plants were infested, and the result was a good crop of cabbage. Whether the sparrows will still continue to merit our praise, in this particular, remains to be seen. Many of our native birds are as partial to this worm as the sparrow, and during my boyhood days always kept them in check, save in seasons when there was an unusual abundance of these pests, and a remarkable falling off in the number of insect-eating birds. Formerly, many caterpillars of the rusty-vaporer moth (*Orgyia leucostigma*) were eaten, but latterly there is little demand for such articles of diet in a region where plenty of other and more agreeable food abounds. During the past season (1877), scarcely a caterpillar of this species was touched. I have observed caterpillars in such places that they could not have escaped detection by the sparrows, but there was apparent a want of disposition to meddle with these irritating creatures. The condition of our Philadelphia squares, and the Common, and public parks of Boston, according to the testimony of H. A. Purdie, Esq., during the summer of 1877, abundantly testify to the truth of my assertion. To the disgust of persons of delicate nerves and sensitive natures, these insect-pests were creeping everywhere. To be sure our numerous measuring worms, many of whose technical names are given above, are still devoured, but through careful watchfulness I am convinced that the rage for these smooth-skinned loopers is a thing of the past. Numbers will still be continued to be fed to the young birds while they are nestlings, but these will be mingled with other diet of a vegetal character.

Dipterous insects, but chiefly in the mature state, are greedily eaten when procurable. To capture these creatures requires no little skill and address. Still I have witnessed such feats by the sparrows, but there was lacking that inimitable precision which characterizes the *Muscicapidæ*, *Vireonidæ*, and to a slight degree, the *Sylvicolidæ*. From the exceedingly limited supply of dipterous food which these birds are able to procure, it is obvious that we cannot look to them to rid man of many of his most inveterate tormentors. The principal insects of this order that are preyed upon are the common house fly (*Musca domestica*), stable fly (*Stomoxys calcitrans*), white-lined horse-fly (*Tabanus lincola*), mosquito (*Culex tæniorhynchus*).

In addition to the foregoing, our various species of *Aphidæ* and *Coccidæ*, are exterminated in countless myriads. Perhaps the good which they accomplish in the destruction of these vegetation-destroyers will compensate for the mischief which they commit in other directions. This good quality, however, certainly loses much of its value when brought before the light of investigation. 'Tis true that these rapidly multiplying creatures are held somewhat in check under sparrow domination. But then how much better is the condition of affairs now than in the past? When our smaller native birds were common denizens of our yards and fields, before the introduction of the sparrows, aphides were not more abundant than under the present regime. Any of our numerous insect-eating birds would destroy as many of these pests in a day as the pugnacious and greedy sparrow, and reward us, besides, for the privilege of nesting in our shade and fruit trees, by the most agreeable melodies and winning manners.

The common earthworm (*Lumbricus terrestris*) is also eaten. In the spring and summer when these creatures make their appearance upon the surface on a clear morning after a night of showers, they are instantly beset and made subservient to a keen and vigorous appetite. When the garden soil has been broken up by the spade preparatory to sowing seed, many of these wiry fellows fall ready victims to the sparrow. Unlike the robin, tanager, and others, it has never been observed in the distant fields, gleaning among the upturned clods for the caitiffs which have been exposed to the light of day by the trenchant plough. Other scenes, the budding and blossoming trees, invite its willing labors.

The flight of the sparrow is low, quite irregular, and but slightly sustained. It never flies to a great distance, when disturbed, like many of the *Fringillidæ*. In this particular, it reminds us of the movements of the song sparrow. Its peculiar physique will not admit of prolonged and rapid flight, but evidently points to a type of structure best adapted to non-migratory habits. The acquirement of such habits must certainly beget the most unenviable traits of character. when viewed in connection with the sparrow's excessive salacity and remarkable powers of reproduction. To the same cause must be ascribed the exceeding sociability which it manifests towards its human brethren.

In gleaning for food it is mainly terrestrial in habits. It is only when in quest of caterpillars for its young, and of articles for the gratification of its own peculiar appetite, that it becomes arboreal.

The song of this species, if I may be allowed so to characterize it, judging from a human standpoint, lacks both variety and expression. It is in striking contrast with the song of *Melospiza melodia*, the common song sparrow, and with that of *Spizella pusilla*, the field sparrow. It cannot fail to attract attention by its utter inharmoniousness. Its ordinary call-note may be quite accurately expressed by the monosyllabic *hwi*, which is repeated at somewhat irregular intervals. A simple *twi-che*, the final syllable being repeated quite sharply, is symbolic of anger; while the cry of vexation and disappointment is indicated by *twi-twi-twoo*, *twi-twi-twoo*, uttered in a lively and discordant manner.

If the sparrow possesses any notes during the period of mating different from what it has been heard to emit at other times, the writer is not cognizant of them. If they exist, they must only be appreciable to persons possessed of a more delicate auditory apparatus than the writer can lay claim to. It would seem that this important period is ushered into existence by the same noisy demonstrations, but, if anything, tenfold more pronounced, as mark the sparrow's daily awakening from the sleep of night. The activity, which is then manifest, is more animated. Contentions, the results of amatory influences, are of frequent occurrence. These are mainly due to desires for particular boxes, and not, as is often erroneously supposed, to desires upon the part of particular males for certain females. I have the best of reasons for believing that, in the generality of cases, the same birds pair on each annual return of the season. My own observations upon this species, in certain isolated localities, thoroughly convince me of the truth of the statement. Boxes that were occupied during the breeding-season have been known to afford shelter to the same parent birds during the inclemency of winter. There are times, doubtless, when this condition of things does not prevail.

Mating commences remarkably early, if it may be said to have a beginning at all. The astounding salacity of the sparrow, which surpasses that of any other species, so far as my knowledge will enable me to form a judgment, inclines me to believe that in many cases it is not accomplished at all. I have observed the sexes together, during the warm days of December and January that sometimes occur in our northern winters, displaying the warmest affection and closest attachment for each other. Such feelings beget an ardor of temperament which manifests itself in conjugal embraces. The sexes, in coition during these months, have frequently been encountered. This should not seem such a wonderful affair, when it is borne in mind that preparations for nest-building are frequently made as early as the first week of February.

Usually, the male among animals is the more amorous of the sexes. But in the case of the sparrow, the female is certainly the equal, if not the superior, of her partner, in this respect. I have observed the male in sexual intercourse with his partner as many as twelve times in less than five minutes. Mr. John Strouse, of Germantown, informs me that fifteen expresses the highest number of times that has come under his notice. Others have observed a much smaller, yet equally astounding, number. The peculiar movements of the female at such times, and her not-to-be-misconstrued call, are enough to satisfy the most skeptical that she is a genuine seducer. The male, though generally anxious, does not always obey her summons. From the foregoing statements, it is obvious that sexual intercourse is not always indulged in with a view of propagating the species, but is frequently performed as a mere sensual gratification. The overstimulated life which these birds lead, has doubtless produced that excessive amativeness which is so conspicuous a feature of their character.

Nidification, as previously remarked, commences early, sometimes as early as the first week of April, but usually not before the last week of March, or the beginning of April. The labors of nest-building are mutually shared, both birds working with a perseverance and diligence truly commendatory. The materials out of which the domicile is built, are mostly gathered by the male, his partner attending to their proper adjustment. I have seen more than a single female engaged in assisting the male in such work. In February, 1875, my attention was called to a pair of females and a single male, carrying dried grasses and feathers to a certain tree-hollow. The most perfect good-will and harmony prevailed among the members of this trio. When the weather was unusually severe, labor was suspended, to be resumed on the return of milder climate. Myself and friends anxiously awaited to see what would be the ultimate result of this tripartite covenant, but before the nest had reached completion, from some cause unknown to us, the locality was deserted, and has not since been occupied. Perhaps the odd female was a young bird that had been hatched late in the season, and who, being strongly attached to her parents, had taken this means of proving her filial affection. It might be supposed that, as these sparrows often resort to hollow trees for shelter during the cold days and nights of winter, the aforementioned articles were designed for no other purpose than that of rendering their roosting quarters more comfortable. I grant the plausibility of this explanation. But, then, it is somewhat negatived by the fact that instances are not wanting to prove that these birds do sometimes take advantage of an unusually warm February in obedience to their natural instincts of brood-raising.

In the selection of a locality some birds are not at all particular; but others, again, manifest a predilection for boxes, or hollow trees. The ivy comes in for its share of attention. Scores of birds not only find comfortable shelter in the midst of its network of leaves and branches during the rigors of winter, but also suitable accommodations for nesting purposes. Where the above conveniences are not available, actuated by a true parental instinct, the birds sometimes place their nests between the forked branches of a tree. The maple is not uncommonly selected for this purpose. A case of the kind came under my immediate observation in the summer of 1874.

A nest, which the writer possesses, may be said to constitute a typical structure, when nidification occurs within a tree-cavity. It occupies the hollow branch of an apple tree, and measures fifteen inches in length, and four inches in diameter. Basally, it is composed of a heterogeneous mixture of feathers, grasses, and leaves; and, peripherally, of a thick wall of dry plant-stems, intermingled with feathers of the barnyard fowl. The labor of nidification ordinarily continues from four to five days, when the builders are working under the most favorable auspices.

The nest just described is unusually large, and is the result of several additions to the original structure after each brood-raising. Three broods had been successfully reared within its walls, and at the time of the severance of the limb from the trunk of the tree, preparations for a fourth brood were manifest. From the great depth of its cavity, the labor of removing the befouled materials, which would have been exceedingly arduous and irksome to the birds, was spared; a fresh supply of feathers being carried into it for each successive brood. The preparations for the fourth brood were being made during the last week of August.

Another nest, which was collected late in June, was built between a forked twig of the common swamp maple. It is composed externally of fine and coarse strings from the thickness of twine to that of sewing silk, carpet rags, a few branchlets of *Populus dilatata* or Lombardy poplar, and a modicum of rootlets. Internally, it is lined with a dense stratum of raw cotton. It measures four and a half inches in diameter at the mouth, and has a depth of two and a half inches. The cavity is three inches wide, and one and a half inches deep. The outer materials are far from being tastefully interwoven, and the arrangement displays but little artistic skill. If its present appearance affords any criterion, the cotton had evidently been found *en masse*, and is adjusted pretty much in the identical condition which it presented when first discovered by the birds.

The latter is the only nest of the kind that I have met with. Its structure is somewhat anomalous. But since my discovery, I have well-authenticated instances of other nests having been found in similar positions. Professor Gilbert, of Germantown, has recently called my attention to a nest of this species, which was placed upon a branch, and securely attached thereto. It was protected from above by an arch-like arrangement, which was firmly fastened to the walls of the nest proper, evidently constituting a part of the structure. A nearly circular aperture formed the only doorway by which access could be obtained to the cosy chamber within.

It would seem from the foregoing statement that, when deprived of the covering which nature affords in various ways in the shape of decayed tree-trunks and branches and the matted leaves and vines of the common ivy, or when deprived of the many human contrivances for nesting purposes, these birds obtain the requisite shelter and comfort, in exposed situations, by building roofs to their domiciles. Here, it is obvious, is another proof, in addition to the many which have been recorded from time to time, of the well-known truth that the actions of the feathered creation are controlled by a reason, similar in kind but different in degree, from that which inspires human motives, and governs human actions. Here is evidence of a high mentality.

Does the sparrow occupy the same nest any two consecutive years together, or does it, on each annual return of the breeding-season, seek a new locality? I incline to the former belief. When the nest is placed in a box, in many instances, the old and soiled materials are carried out, and a fresh supply takes their place. The comparative ease with which this labor can be accomplished renders it preferable to any other. But in cases where the nest is situated deep down in a hollow tree-branch, the labor of removing the entire materials, especially where the same nest has been made to answer for several broods, would be almost herculean, and is therefore seldom attempted. A few of the upper articles only are removed, and others put into their places. The same site is thus made available for several years, and is only deserted when no longer fitted for duties of incubation and brood-raising.

When the ivy is taken possession of for nesting and roosting purposes, for it must be remembered that there is a decided preference for this vine as evidenced by the hundreds of birds that avail themselves of its shelter, there is good reason for believing that the same nest is occupied until it becomes so rotten and time-worn as to drop from its moorings, when the unfortunate owners are compelled to construct another. Like the robin, the sparrow always makes the necessary repairs to its home, which have been rendered necessary by the war of elements to which it has been subjected. But, in the generality of cases, it is otherwise with the robin; it follows the example of its great brotherhood of birds in constructing a new nest on each recurrence of the nesting-season.

The labors of nidification being accomplished, but little time is wasted in celebrating this remarkable event. The birds seem actuated by the most intense desire to obey the controlling instinct of their being, the chief aim of their transitory existence. Consequently, oviposition commences on the day succeeding nest-completion. The eggs are deposited not oftener than one a day. The ordinary complement is not less than four, nor more than five. Incubation immediately succeeds oviposition, in the majority of instances, and is never later than the day following the last deposit. It continues for eleven days. The burden of the responsibility devolves chiefly upon the female, although the male does not refuse his generous assistance. While his partner is thus occupied, he is a faithful guardian, and willing provider. He exhibits great affection for her, and is indefatigable in his efforts to render her comfortable and happy. His jealousy is unbounded. No feathered stranger is permitted within his territory, without receiving summary and condign punishment for such temerity. When unable to cope with the enemy, a call-note of distress brings scores of friends to the rescue. He seldom strays any considerable distance from home, except when foraging. He maintains the most friendly relations with his neighbors, and is seldom known to violate the rules of common decency and good faith. He never trespasses upon the rights and property of a friend, and is extremely jealous of his own. Matrimonial relations are entered into with a due sense of their honor and sacredness. In not a single instance have I known a real flirtation to be practised, a genuine case of desertion by either sex, or one of infidelity. The remarkable salacity which characterizes the social life of this species, one would suppose, would break up the harmony which exists, and turn a well-regulated and peaceful community into a state of society where quarrels and bitter animosities would be of daily occurrence; in fine, would convert it into a communism, or a state of society in which polygamy would be a prevailing feature. Like our common *Gallus*, the most powerful males would be the more highly favored. But, be it said to the credit of the species, a more perfect pattern of conjugal faithfulness could scarcely be pictured to the mind. Its extreme amativeness is doubtless, as before remarked, the result of the overstimulated life which these birds lead in the land of their forced adoption. Although induced by climatic and dietetic causes, which act with greater freedom and power here than in the land of its nativity, as I infer from the silence of European writers upon the subject, it is gratifying and consoling to reflect that the change has not been so radical as to operate towards the destruction of the social ties which bind the individuals of this species into a harmonious whole, and which has cemented a friendship so strong and durable that infidelity is out the question.

The extraordinary degree of affection which the sexes display towards each other, naturally leads to the inference that parental love lacks naught of the power and vigor of conjugal love. We therefore find that the most devoted affection and the greatest concern are manifested for the young. Both parents vie with each other in rendering them every needful attention. To satisfy their voracious appetites, they are kept alternately busy from morning until night, as well by cloudy and rainy, as by fair and sunshiny weather. Occasionally, both birds are absent from home on this important business. When with young, should the nest be assailed by human or feathered foe, the utmost excitement, and the most deafening din, prevail. In the case of a feathered enemy, the combined vengeance of the insulted pair is wreaked upon the daring and presumptuous offender. In these attacks, the female is the compeer of her lord. It is seldom that, except in isolated cases, the necessity for such assaults exists, for, where the requisite accommodations abound, a disposition to dwell in communities is manifest, and few species have the rashness to attempt any molestation.

When the young have attained the age of from twelve to thirteen days, they quit the nest, but are still fed by the parents from ten to eleven days longer, when they are sufficiently matured to shift for themselves. Parental affection permits them to linger about their homes, and where conveniences exist, they are allowed to seek shelter, during inclement weather and winter nights, in the boxes and hollows which served them as nests during their helpless stage of existence.

Generally, three broods are annually raised. Instances are known to the writer where preparations were making for a fourth brood, when the designs of the birds were frustrated by human interference.

During the prevalence of cold weather, at nights, and even in the warmer seasons of the year, in the daytime when the rain is descending in torrents, almost any convenience is appropriated for roosting purposes. Hollow trees, ivy vines, boxes, eaves of buildings, and outhouses, are common places of resort. In rural districts, barracks and haystacks afford cosy and comfortable quarters.

In some portions of Philadelphia immense numbers take refuge in the ivy. In the writer's neighborhood, especially upon the north side of the mansion of Mr. John Button, carefully protected from cold winds and pelting storms by surrounding dwellings, within an extensive vine which covers the entire gable-end, at least a hundred sparrows find comfortable lodgings. The ceaseless clatter which the birds produce during early morning, and in the evening, is almost deafening. During the breeding-period, the vine is literally filled with nests. In asserting that fifty pairs and upward nidificate within its limits, the writer cannot be accused of misrepresentation or exaggeration. Notwithstanding the petty quarrels which sometimes occur, especially in the spring, a high degree of harmony prevails. May this not be accounted for by the fact that this entire community is the natural outgrowth of a single pair that took up its quarters in the vine several years ago?

The eggs of the house sparrow are oval, pointed at one extremity, and dotted with various shades of cinereous brown upon a light ashen background. Their average length is .91 of an inch, and average breadth .62.

The breeding-period being over, both old birds and young may often be seen together, dusting themselves in the streets (for which they show great fondness), or else be observed upon a freshly deposited heap of horse-dung, gorging themselves to satiety upon the undigested fragments of grain and other substances which it contains. Often, on such occasions, have we remarked the attention which the parent birds bestow upon their numerous progeny, showing their affection by the tender of some racy article which they have discovered in their careful and diligent examination.

Even at this period, and all along through the dreary autumnal and winter months which follow, owing to the extreme scarcity of suitable roosting quarters, which is mainly noticeable within large towns and cities in consequence of the vast abundance of these birds, immense numbers seek shelter upon window ledges, and underneath verandas or porches, which they defile by their disgusting habits. The heaps of excrement which they leave in such places, a sorry compensation for the kindness and benevolence which tolerate their presence, are considerable. To the tidy and careful housewife, they are unmitigated nuisances. It is not surprising that many should place them under the ban of excommunication, and whenever the opportunity is afforded, should persecute them with a bitter hatred. In the country, a similar complaint prevails; but there the mischief done to newly-painted cornices, pillars, and window-ledges, is small in comparison with what is accomplished by these feathered denizens in cities.

In concluding this rather imperfect sketch of the sparrow, I cannot refrain from mentioning a few facts gleaned from other sources. In the winter of 1875, James Kirk, Esq., of Germantown, informs me that he erected a rather capacious house with several compartments, for the accommodation of these birds, which were frequent visitants to his garden. Every encouragement was given to them to build. Although the house was put up long before the commencement of the breeding-period, to my informant's surprise, not a single pair of birds could be induced to take permanent possession. Unable to solve the problem, application for a solution was made to the writer. A little conversation with the gentleman elicited a number of facts which, associated with others that had come under the writer's observation, enabled the latter to solve the question. It was apparent from the above conversation, that several attempts had been made by different parties to build, but owing to the unfriendly relations which subsisted between them, they all proved failures. Others had attempted it with the same results. Experience has taught the writer that when houses and even vines are occupied by birds of near kinship, but few if any difficulties occur to mar the happiness of the occupants; but, on the contrary, when different clans, so to speak, come together, more or less jangling is the certain and unavoidable result. In view of these established truths, I will be safe in concluding that, however suitable my friend's building may have been for nidificating purposes, for the sparrow, like our common house wren (*Troglodytes aedon*), is not at all fastidious in its selection of a house, its abandonment was solely due to the conflicting natures of the parties that sought to possess it.

Some interesting observations, showing the reprehensible conduct of the sparrow, have lately appeared in the "Hartford Times" bearing date Oct. 17, 1877. As a general thing, I care very little for newspaper science, but these facts are so good, and correspond so closely with notes of others and my own, and are such that we should expect from the known character of this species, that I cannot refrain from giving them further publicity. The story was given on the authority of a friend of the writer's, who obtained it direct from the person that witnessed the occurrences. This gentleman, a resident of New York, had erected in his backyard, during the spring of 1877, a large box for the accommodation of the sparrows. It was so constructed that twelve pairs of birds could find appropriate quarters for nesting. These apartments were soon appropriated, and the business of the season proceeded "amid the chippering din of these fussy and pugnacious feathered colonists." Sitting idly at his window one Sunday observing the busy creatures, the gentleman's attention was arrested by a cock-sparrow which came flying to his place with a fine soft white feather in his bill. The position of the box was such that he could look into the compartments. In this case the bird was observed to deposit the feather into an incomplete nest, and then fly away. No sooner had he disappeared, than the nest was visited by a female sparrow from the adjoining compartment who had evidently noticed the proceeding, and the coveted feather was carried away. Instead of carrying the stolen article to her own nest, she made off with the feather to a neighboring tree, where she securely fastened it, in an inconspicuous place, upon and between two twigs. There she left it and returned home. Pretty soon the loser came back with a straw to add to his nest. Discovering his loss, he issued out, and with many an angry expostulation, vowed vengeance upon the despoiler of his home. His first demonstration was to visit his next door neighbor, but finding no trace of the pilfered feather, somewhat perplexed, he retired, and desisting from further attempts at discovery, flew away in quest of another. The guilty party, after innocently and loudly demanding a reason for this ungentlemanly intrusion in order to turn suspicion away from herself, as soon as her offended neighbor had got well out of sight, flew to the tree, seized the stolen feather, and bore it triumphantly to her own nest.

Mr. Elliott, in his Birds of North America, mentions a rather curious incident, which goes far to show the familiar and curious disposition of the sparrow. It savors somewhat of the ludicrous, but is sufficiently interesting to be given. In August, 1868, while passing by an undertaker's shop in Jersey City, his attention was attracted to one of these birds which was hopping very quietly about in a glass window that had been left open, intently inspecting the caskets on exhibition, doubtless with the view of selecting one in which to construct a nest.

A writer, in the "Scientific American" for August 11, 1877, mentions a few observations concerning these birds which had previously escaped the writer's attention. But since their perusal, I have been able to confirm them. He not only calls notice to a change of habit which this species has undergone, but also to a change of color. His observations are wholly restricted to New York City and its environs. While a sparrow with a white feather would be considered much of a curiosity in England or France, says substantially our informant, such birds are by no means uncommon in and about that city. According to this writer they constitute at least five per cent. of the entire number. In the City Hall Park, and at Bloomingdale, birds are frequently seen with unusually light plumage. In the midst of Germantown, I have observed at least five birds out of every hundred, in which this color-change was decidedly manifest. Further, our informant says, after comparing the movements of the European sparrow with those of its cis-Atlantic cousin, that the former moves with a clear and distinct hop, thus making a quite perceptible pause between the two consecutive hops; while the latter makes a succession of quick hops with very small ascent, almost equivalent to a short run, then stops very abruptly, thus resembling, in a measure, the characteristic movement of the American robin. In conclusion, he says that the American bird is seemingly " entertaining somewhat of disdain for the insectivorousness to which he owes his importation, forgetful that in no other way can he pay his passage money."

It is well known that the most friendly relations subsist among the sparrows of the same household. Instances have been recorded showing this, and also the willingness and readiness with which they hasten to the rescue of one of their number when in danger.

How they will deport themselves when a comrade is ill, I cannot say from experience; but a knowledge of the social life of this species, in many of its different phases, amply qualifies me to speak. But I am debarred from hazarding an opinion. The New York "Sun" has called attention to a case in point which occurred quite recently. In the Jersey City ferry-house of the Pavonia Ferry, a flock of sparrows excited much interest among the passengers, in their endeavors to take care of a companion who was evidently sick. After much chippering among the birds, as though they had been holding a consultation, it was finally settled to put the patient behind the top cornice of a pillar. The sick bird was then borne to the chosen spot by three of its companions, and carefully covered over with straw. Everything having passed off quite satisfactorily, a dozen sparrows perched upon the telegraph wire, and in loud vociferations celebrated the success of the difficult undertaking.

The human-like and orderly execution of this business, leads me to suspect that a leader of superior intelligence and wisdom directed the whole affair. In the absence of any positive information bearing upon the subject, I am led to this belief from facts which have come into my possession since commencing this article. William Kenney, Esq., of this place, informs me that he has given considerable attention to the sparrows, which frequent his trees and ivy vines in large numbers, nesting in the hollows of the trees, and roosting in the vines. He asserts that their noise in the early evening is almost deafening, each bird endeavoring to outstrip its companions in vocal demonstrations. All appear to be in the full enjoyment of happiness. But after a half hour thus spent, one of the birds is observed to leave the vine, and by a given signal, so loud as to be distinctly heard by all, commands silence. The order is instantly obeyed, and quietness reigns supreme. Mr. Kenney assures me that he has seen the movements, and heard the call, on scores of occasions, and cannot be mistaken.

CHAPTER III.

EVIDENCE, BOTH POSITIVE AND NEGATIVE, OF THE SPARROW'S USEFULNESS IN AMERICA.

In the very imperfect sketch which I have given of the sparrow's life in its American home, which is mainly based upon my own observations, I would be guilty of manifest injustice to my contemporaries who have written upon the subject, if I should omit to make mention of their writings and discoveries. Besides, I would be neglecting a duty which I owe as well to myself as to them. The value of confirmatory evidence cannot be adequately appreciated. The evidence which I have to offer, therefore, will be both of an affirmative and of a negative character.

In the Annals of the Lyceum of Natural History for 1867, Mr. Lawrence has given a brief sketch of the sparrow's introduction, and of the benefits which had accrued therefrom to society up to the time of his writing. He says, "The pest of our shade trees and horrors of pedestrians (caterpillars of *Ennomos subsignaria*) form part of the diet of this species."

Dr. Charles Pickering, who had obviously given considerable attention to the study of the sparrow-question, in the Proceedings of the Boston Society for 1867, cites several authorities to show that these birds have been the enemies of mankind for more than 5000 years. At the period of the invention of writing this bird, according to Mr. Pickering, was selected "as the hieroglyphic character signifying enemy." This writer was led into his investigations of its past history only after noticing exhibitions of its pugnacious disposition, and destructive character, in his native city of Boston.

In the Proclamation of the Boston Society for 1869, Dr. Brewer speaks of the good which the sparrows have accomplished in New York, in the destruction of the measuring worms of that city, and neighboring cities. In the summer of 1867, he remarks, they were observed actively engaged over the city in clearing trees of worms, and so successfully, that the foliage of none was known to be eaten. Great hopes were entertained by him of the incalculable services which they would render to this country, not merely in keeping measuring worms, but also canker worms, caterpillars, and possibly curculio in check. In the work entitled "North American Birds," his earliest views, the results of his own observations, are doubtless expressed. Read what he says :—

"Apprehensions have been expressed that these new-comers may molest and drive away our own native birds. How this may be when the sparrows become more numerous cannot now be determined, but so far they manifest no such disposition. Since their introduction into Boston, the chipping sparrows appear to have increased, and to associate by preference with their European visitors, feeding with them unmolested. I have been unable to detect a single instance in which they have been molested in any manner by their larger companions."

In September's issue of the "American Naturalist" for 1874, in answer to a small article which was published in a previous number, in which Dr. Coues sets forth some remarks of the writer's that are derogatory to the sparrow's character, occurs the following pointed declaration:—

"They never molest, attack, or try to drive away any birds except their own species, and that only from amatory influences. In such times the males are pugnacious against other males of their own species, but nothing more. The females are not at all pugnacious under any circumstances."

In a subsequent issue of the above journal (Oct. 1874), a lengthy reply from the pen of the writer is recorded. In it occurs evidence of the sparrow's irritable, and above all, pugnacious disposition, substantiated by the observations of Messrs. Abel Willis, John Strouse, and others of Germantown, Pa. The same number contains an article from the pen of Mr. Stephen Gould, of Newport, R. I., corroborative of Dr. Brewer's statements. This writer claims that the house sparrow is nearly always accompanied by the American goldfinch and our common sparrow, and actually fraternizes with the blackbirds; in short, courts the society of other birds rather than seeks to drive them away. The male birds only, he affirms, "fight among themselves after the manner of roosters, but do not seem to molest other birds."

As early as 1874, in this country, do we discover that the sparrows are not as destructive to insects as was at first supposed. None will deny that they have been of service. For several years prior to their introduction, the measuring worms preyed upon the leaves of trees to such an extent that, when summer dawned, scarcely a tree was to be seen that had not been rifled of its foliage. So effectively had the sparrows accomplished their labors that, two years subsequent to their introduction, hardly a worm was to be seen. Early in 1874, according to the "Medical Times," another insect foe made its appearance, in the shape of the caterpillar of the rusty-vaporer moth, the *Orgyia leucostigma* of entomologists. As long as the measuring worms were permitted to rest undisturbed, this caterpillar, which comes rather late, discovered the "struggle for existence" a sharp one, its natural provisions being consumed by the worm. It now finds an ample supply of food, and, consequently, is flourishing and increasing rapidly in numbers. Its hairy integument protects it in a great measure from the sparrow's assaults. Some other bird must be found to exterminate this pest. But inasmuch as the sparrow is a very obstinate and pugnacious little fellow, it is doubtful whether he will permit a stranger to trespass upon his territory. The writer referred to above, says, "At present, very many trees in this city have again put on the familiar woe-begone look of old, hiding their misery with the merest tatters and shreds of leaves. But the new-comer doesn't drop on you? Doesn't he though? If he does not drop, he crawls, or gets on some way or other, and the man who has felt his long hairs tickling his neck, struck for a fly, and finds in his hand a bare and bursted carcass, on his shirt collar a stain, and down his back a bunch of tickling hairs, will vote the 'survival of the fittest,' in its latest form, an unmitigated nuisance."

At the meeting of the American Association, held August, 1875, Dr. John L. Le Conte, of Philadelphia, asserts that the sparrow does not attack the larva of *Orgyia leucostigma*, being doubtless deterred therefrom by the bristles with which it is protected.

From this period to the spring of 1877, very little was written about the sparrow, excepting the writer's work on the Birds of Eastern Pennsylvania. The many unenviable traits of character which this species possesses were nevertheless matters of daily observation and conversation. After Dr. Brewer's return from Europe, where he had been making a rather protracted visit, the sparrow-question is again revived, and these much-abused and scandalized creatures find a firm friend and staunch defender. In the Washington Gazette, bearing date June, 1877, the doctor substantially affirms that robins were more plentiful in Boston than ever before, being ten times more numerous than they were a decade since; that bluebirds now abound, which were recently unknown; that white-bellied swallows, chipping sparrows, and purple martins have appeared in legions; and, finally, that "each year adds new species, even such forest-birds as the yellow-bellied woodpecker."

In "The American Cultivator" for August, 1877, similar views are expressed by this indefatigable writer, clinched by the opinions of John Galvin, Esq., the City Forester of Boston.

The last-named gentleman, in reply to certain questions which were submitted to him by Dr. Brewer, April 23, 1877, affirms without hesitation that "the sparrows do not molest or interfere with any other bird. They do not trouble the robin or bluebird, or manifest any animosity against either. All summer long they are together, and it would be impossible for this to be done without my men or I noticing it, yet I never witnessed anything of the kind."

"I have not noticed any decrease in the numbers of any kind, but, on the contrary, a very marked increase of various kinds. The robins were more numerous on the Common last summer than ever before. The little chip-sparrow has become very numerous, and seems to be very fond of the sparrow, often feeding on the same bit of bread. The small martins have very greatly increased in numbers on account of the number of boxes. These they take possession of whenever they want one, and drive the sparrows away. Before the sparrows came there were no bluebirds at all. Now they are becoming quite common, and often treat the sparrows very badly, taking away from them their boxes and breaking up their nests. The sparrows, of course, show fight, but the bluebirds are always too strong for them."

"I am all in favor of the sparrows. I believe that they do no harm, but a great deal of good. Thousands of dollars would not pay the city for their loss, and I would be very sorry to see anything done to prejudice people against them or permit their destruction."

Again, the same writer, in clear and unmistakable language, says, "Their introduction into Boston was immediately attended with great benefit, almost beyond calculation. The trees on the Common were infested with a nasty yellow caterpillar, which destroyed the leaves and buds of the elms and other trees; and these insects increased very rapidly in spite of all that my men could do to destroy them, and, at the south end, the elm trees were eaten every June by swarms of canker-worms. Both of these pests have been pretty nearly exterminated," etc.

Negativing the assertions of Messrs. Brewer and Galvin, we have the unequivocal statements of H. D. Minot, Esq., of Cambridge, Mass. This gentleman, who is distinguished alike for the scope and accuracy of his observations, remarks in a late number of the "Forest and Stream," in giving his objections to the English sparrow: "1. They have no personal attractions, except their tameness. 2. They are practically useless, and are no longer needed. In Cambridge, those trees which are properly tarred have no canker-worms on them, because the female moth is wingless, and, if prevented from ascending the trunk, cannot lay her eggs near leaf-buds. Many others of the elms here are largely stripped, but I have not seen an English sparrow eat one canker-worm, though both the birds and caterpillars are abundant. The birds may have been useful on their first arrival from Europe, but they are too much pampered to be so now, at least to any satisfactory extent. 3. They destroy fruit blossoms. 4. They are often quarrelsome, and sometimes drive away other useful birds, as I can positively testify to from my personal observation."

H. A. Purdie, Esq., of Boston, whose reliability as an ornithologist is unquestioned, in a communication to the "Boston Daily Advertiser," July 30, 1877, confirms Mr. Minot's statements in part. He says, "All over the boles of the elms, maples, lindens, and other trees might be seen crawling the larvæ or caterpillars of the tussock, plumed or vaporer moth, also known as the white-marked orgyia, *Orgyia leucostigma*. They had descended from the branches where since May they have been feeding, and many were spinning about themselves their temporary home or cocoon. In a few days the completed cocoons were to be seen by thousands," etc.

Then, in reply to some rather sweeping assertions which appeared in the columns of the "Journal and Transcript," and "Forest and Stream," in which the writer asserts that "here in Boston the sulphur-colored caterpillars have ceased to disgust us with their odious presence, and we no longer fear for the safety of our elms as we did in 1869," etc., Mr. Purdie inquires, "Why these caterpillars on our trees? With more sparrows than ever before, and more native species, how can it be? These crawling things come from eggs that all last fall, winter, and spring, the pretty little sparrows should have eaten. They were laid by the wingless female imago, which should also have been devoured. The chrysalis must now be swallowed as a dainty morsel! But no; not one is molested by *Passer domesticus*."

Still further our informant remarks: "Mr. Galvin must have noticed this and re-engaged his corps of tree-scrapers, for on the 18th instant, men appeared on the Common, each armed with a sharp-pointed pole with which then and since they destroyed the caterpillars and their cocoons, and the trees bear scars where each victim was effectively impaled. But those within ground-reach only are disposed of. Others on the limbs of the larger trees are left for the sparrows to enjoy. In a week or two more the transformation will be complete, the male moths will be seen flying about, and the unobserved female, simply crawling from the inside to the outside of her cocoon, will there deposit her eggs, the same to develop next season into the destructive stage of existence."

Mr. Purdie does not leave the subject here. After showing that the trees of the Common are provided with one or more occupied boxes to each tree, he leaves the scene and invites the reader to a place on Bowdoin Street, where stand six trees, maples and horse-chestnuts, nearly destitute of foliage. In one of these trees are two boxes, and in three of the others, one box each, and although the occupants are close at hand and have raised one or two broods in each of the boxes, yet the trunks and branches of the trees, as well as the boxes themselves, are completely covered by cocoons. In speaking of the scarcity of our smaller native birds in the same article, Mr. Purdie says, "I have been on the Common nearly every day, and less often on the public garden, for the past ten years, and have been a close observer, and have kept a list of the native species noticed. I am sorry to say, for I wish it were otherwise, that our birds have wonderfully decreased in both species and numbers. I miss their songs and other notes. The big robin I except; that bouncer of the sod holds his own against all odds. Who has caused this thing, but the pugnacious *fringilla*, now courted by the city?"

Mr. Deane, also a resident of Boston, who is no less remarkable for the extent than the accuracy of his observations, bears indubitable testimony to the truth of the foregoing assertions.

Dr. Coues, one of the leaders of ornithology in this country, a gentleman who has done more to advance this favorite branch of science than possibly any one else, in the "Field and Forest" for May, remarks that, "*Passer domesticus*, the nuisance, was introduced some years after our last appeared, and now these rowdy little *gamins* squeak and fight all through the city to our great disgust. The introduction of these exotics clutters up ornithology in a way that a student of geographical distribution may deplore, and interferes decidedly with the balance of power among the native species. Whatever may be said to the contrary notwithstanding, these sparrows do molest, harass, drive off, and otherwise maltreat and forcibly eject and attempt to destroy various kinds of native birds, which are thereby deprived of certain inalienable rights to life, liberty, and the pursuit of happiness after their own fashion."

In the "Chicago Field" for July, 1877, we have another article from the same gifted pen. After alluding to the introduction of the sparrows into this country, the good which they were expected to accomplish, their remarkable increase, and a dozen no less interesting matters, the doctor is at length brought to the main point which he has to urge against these birds, namely, the reaction of their presence upon our native birds. He remarks that,—

"They are rapidly exterminating the native songsters and insect-eating birds from our cities, and what the result will be when the sparrows overflow into all the country, even I, who try to be alive to the whole case, can only imagine. The sparrows are lusty, vigorous birds, remarkably stout for their size, and withal most pugnacious, irascible, irritable creatures, who wage perpetual warfare with the peacably disposed and unoffending birds with whom they are necessarily thrown into contact. This is contact of a kind that necessarily implies competition, and in every struggle for existence, as we all know, the weakest must go to the wall."

In the "Forest and Stream" for June, 1877, a very interesting article bearing upon the much mooted "sparrow question," appears from the pen of William Walsh, Esq., of Brooklyn, N. Y. The writer, after speaking about the warfare which these birds wage upon the bluebird, robin, wren, and worst of all upon that "sweet charmer of the spring," the song sparrow; their utter uselessness in the destruction of the rose-bug and a species of green worm, and their peculiar penchant for cherries, concludes his interesting sketch in the following language:—

"From what I have seen I know from experience that the sparrow is a good-for-nothing, domineering bird, and any casual observer cannot help but notice that they are always fighting among themselves, and if one picks up a crumb or worm the others pursue him to the death almost, to take it away, and more times than one have I seen him drop a 'rare bit' trying to flee from his companions. They let orchards go to ruin, for they will not eat every kind of insect, and the cornices and window tops of the houses in our cities present a disgraceful sight from their droppings, they preferring to build their nest in the eaves of houses and spend their time among dung hills in the street, rather than protect the orchards, which they were transported for. They are given to wanton laziness, and I recommend that the Acclimatization Society ship them all home again, and bring English starlings, nightingales, and the like, and while they are about it, bring over some English partridge and woodcock."

J. H. Batty, Esq., of New Utrecht, N. Y., than whom no better authority upon the sparrow exists in that State, has placed upon record the history of its pugnacious disposition and destructive propensities.

H. G. Carey, Esq., of Indianapolis, Ia., although a warm friend to the sparrow, in the midst of the many excellent things which he says about the species, for examples, their wholesale destruction of noxious insects, and the friendly relations which they have established with our native birds, consistently affirms,—

"Their value as a means of defence against the ravages of insects and worms upon foliage and plants, is in an inverse ratio to the amount of other food at their command. If there is an abundance of grain and offal suited to their tastes, at their disposal, they will not exert themselves in search of worms. They get in their best work on insects and caterpillars by destroying their larvæ during the winter season when other means of subsistence are scarce."

Again:—

" They prefer to build their nests in small boxes placed fifteen or twenty feet above the ground on trees in public streets, walks, or grounds. When a sufficient number of these is not supplied, they will build in hollow cornices, brackets, window caps, or in projections of any character on the walls, or under the eaves of houses— always selecting the front or most public exposure. In these localities they, from their noise and droppings, often become great sources of annoyance."

An anonymous writer, in "Forest and Stream" for May, 1877, writes in disparaging terms of the sparrow's usefulness. After alluding to its introduction into Indianapolis for the purposes of " worming" and " bugging," the writer says,—

" From less than a hundred they are now become thousands, and still the caterpillar swings its nest on the elm and pear tree. The miller flits in undiminished numbers about the evening lamps. In fact, it is believed that these foreigners are mere scavengers, alighting upon the streets, and eating offal with our common pigeons."

In New York City and surroundings, evidence of the sparrow's jealous disposition and destructive propensities, is not wanting. In an anonymous article to the "Forest and Stream" for June, 1877, a few thoughts as to the advisability of permitting these birds to increase in their present alarming proportion, are given. The writer, after alluding to the eminent service which they perform in the destruction of the insects which prey upon the foliage of trees, in municipal districts, and in the removal of refuse materials, argues that we can very well dispense with the few birds which were accustomed to visit such localities before the introduction of the former. He, then, after a brief allusion to the verdict of Mr. Galvin, of Boston, says in unequivocal language:

"Where the English sparrows congregate or breed in numbers, there soon our native birds are wanting. We have time and again witnessed the fierce pugnacity of the imported birds. Among themselves they are exceedingly quarrelsome, but let a bird of a different genus but show himself, and the fury of the whole sparrow community is turned upon the helpless interloper: they chase him hither and thither, giving him no rest until he is banished from the neighborhood. The sparrows prefer the city streets, where their repulsive food is plenty, and select the public parks for breeding, but their marvellous increase has driven hordes of them out to the surrounding suburbs, where their presence is not needed, the numberless insectivorous and worm-eating natives generally being there amply sufficient to cope with the vermin. We have in mind a locality on the banks of the Hudson, not many miles from the heart of New York City, a spot noted for its forest trees and picturesque loveliness. A very few years ago it was the abiding place of many of our most melodious song birds. The wood-thrush sent his metallic notes ringing from the tall oak and hemlock; the robin, scarlet tanager, oriole, and a host of others, made the woods ring with their songs, or enlivened the scene with their brilliant plumage."

"The English sparrow, overflowing from the city, made his ill-omened appearance; within six months, the harsh never-ceasing chirp filled the air from morning until night, and our native birds began to be heard and seen in less numbers. The following spring the most prized wood-thrush had gone elsewhere to breed, and there was a corresponding diminution in the number of our other yearly visitants. The indignation of the neighbors soon vented itself on the useless usurpers, and they were, by being killed and having their nests broken up, soon driven off, and at the present time, two years since the banishment of the English birds, the native and aboriginal avi-fauna of that region is as plentiful as it ever was."

The editor of the last-mentioned journal, in his issue for July, 1877, prints two very interesting and graceful contributions to the sparrow-question, from the pens of lady correspondents who, according to his statement, are " direct descendants of the man who, during the early days of American scientific research, did perhaps more than any one before or since has done for the advancement of its interests. They come from those living on the spot where the immortal artist naturalist spent some of his happiest years; where, having accomplished his great life-work, he passed into a ripe old age, then peacefully away." It requires but little effort of the mind to imagine to whom the editor refers.

The value of this testimony, coming as it does from persons who have doubtless inherited much from their illustrious ancestor, cannot be fully appreciated, and must certainly be treated by the friends of the sparrow, with a due degree of reverence and respect. The first lady, writing from New York City, over a rather euphonious cognomen, says, concerning the advisability of cultivating the English sparrow,—

"I deem it not only a pleasure to add my testimony against them, but a duty, to use every means in my power to aid those who desire to banish to the city the little pests, as much the enemies of our birds as ever tories were of whigs."

Then, after briefly alluding to the reason which the defendants of these birds give for allowing them to increase, namely, their destruction of the worms which infest trees and vegetables, she says,—

"Can it be that they do not know that our native birds do the same? In a city where the latter will not live, the sparrow may have his work to do, but certainly in no other place, and for no other reason could any one ever care to raise them, for they are neither handsome nor songsters. That they do drive away all other birds from any locality which is so unfortunate as to have them for inhabitants is to me, and any close observer, an indisputable fact. Some years ago, several of the neighbors brought large numbers of them to this place. In an incredibly short time not a forest bird was to be seen or heard. This was borne impatiently for a year or so, until the guns of more than one lover of justice and friend to the birds, drove the usurpers from the place. Since their banishment the forest birds have returned in full force, and once more their sweet notes are heard around the home of him who made the study of them and their habits his life-work."

The other anonymous communication to which reference has been made, emanating as it does from the pen of a lady deeply alive to the interest of the subject, is pregnant with the most astounding truths. I cannot refrain from quoting it in its entirety. Read what she says:—

"Let me say a few words for the dear companions of my childhood. I live in one of the loveliest spots on earth, on the banks of the Hudson. Magnificent old forest trees surround me while I write, and the songs of many birds fill my heart with their melody. To my mind, their notes this afternoon have a pleading tone, and I feel compelled to answer their appeal by using my small influence against their enemies, the sparrows. Years ago our ears were delighted with the thrilling notes of the thrush, the meadow lark, the oriole, and many birds who find a welcome home in our grand old pines and oaks. We little thought when we welcomed as enthusiastically as any one the importance of the sparrow that they would destroy this pleasure for us; but sad experience has taught us a lesson regarding them. As they accomplished their work so well in the city, it was deemed advisable to try them here also; why, I know not, as I cannot remember that we were ever much troubled in our locality with the worms and caterpillars that did, I know, infest New York. But out they came in great numbers, and bitterly did we rue the day. One by one our dear little songsters disappeared, larks, thrushes, scarlet tanagers, orioles, all fell victims to the quarrelsome dispositions of the little sparrows. Even the robins could hardly hold their own against them. For three or four years we suffered the loss of our favorites, and then indignation overpowered us, and we rose in a body to drive the intruders away. We have done so almost entirely, and this summer, for the first time in many years, have again welcomed our native birds, but if we are to keep them we must destroy the sparrows, as they do most certainly fight and kill all other birds. Let them keep to the city, where they have done, and are doing, a good work, but leave us in our country homes our own feathered songsters."

In the summer of 1877, the writer spent considerable time in New York City, Jersey City, Newark, and several other large towns and cities of the State of New Jersey where the sparrows are quite plentiful, and observed on scores of occasions, exhibitions of their insolent bearing towards our native birds, particularly towards such as remained. The great scarcity of the latter was a rather noticeable feature. H. H. Rusby, Esq., of Franklin, N. J., who accompanied me in my travels, can testify to the truth of my statement. The same close observer assured me that he had frequently witnessed the unprovoked assaults of the sparrows upon our native birds, and the persistence with which they were continued. From numerous observations he said "he had become convinced that there existed a feeling of hatred towards our native species, which invariably manifested itself when the latter came into contact therewith." He further assured the writer that our own birds decreased *pari passu* with the increase and spread of the foreigners. Concerning the destructiveness of the sparrows, Mr. Rusby says, "Farmers in the vicinity of Newark, N. J., have been seriously troubled during the past season (1877) by the depredations of the sparrows upon the growing corn. These birds, gathering in the hedges and along the fence-rows, often make inroads upon the field to the distance of two rods, and tearing open the husks at the end of the ear, devour the young corn. I have seen fields where the grain near the borders was almost entirely destroyed, and have heard farmers predict that the time would come when the raising of Indian corn would be rendered almost impossible, owing to this pernicious influence." Evidence of a similar character from localities occupied by the sparrows, in divers parts of New Jersey, could be adduced, but the desire not to protract this chapter beyond certain limits, prevents the author from a recital of numerous authorities. He will, therefore, mention one other authority from this section of the country, and pass to evidence of the sparrow's fighting and destructive qualities, as witnessed in Eastern Pennsylvania.

Prof. Cope, a naturalist of rare attainments, and remarkable alike for the extent and correctness of his observations, informs the writer that while a resident of Haddonfield, N. J., where these birds are exceedingly abundant, incessant warfare was waged upon all the smaller birds that dared to intrude upon occupied territory, the fox sparrow (*Passerella iliaca*) alone being able to cope with the stranger. Even the robin, which is generally able to hold its own, according to the same eminent authority, was compelled to retreat before the inveterate attacks of these invaders.

From Philadelphia and its environs, the testimonies of a score and even more of observers could be given concerning the sparrow's uselessness. The great body of evidence is derogatory to its character. I know of no competent witness that could be brought forward to testify to its general usefulness. To be sure, I could mention a few names of individuals who would so testify, but their evidence must be ruled out, owing to incompetency on the ground of ignorance and national prejudice.

John Strouse, of Chestnut Hill (a suburb of Philadelphia), can testify to the truth of the foregoing assertions. In a conversation with the writer upon the sparrow's usefulness, he says:—

"The chipping sparrow, bluebird, house wren, and great crested flycatcher, were in past years common denizens of my yard and kitchen-garden, and were accustomed to build therein; but now the detestable sparrows have usurped their places. The unprovoked hostilities, which the latter have waged against their unoffending brethren, have induced me to make war upon them. I have generously given our birds that encouragement and protection which a purblind municipality has denied. In the spring, when my grape-vines are in blossom, they are attacked, and scarcely a blossom is left to mature into fruit. Even the latter requires the closest vigilance to prevent its destruction. In other places I have witnessed similar depredations, not only upon the vines, but also upon the blossoms and ripened fruit of the cherry, and the produce of the strawberry and raspberry. In harvest time immense flocks settle down upon the prostrate grain and destroy immense quantities of this staple article of food."

William E. Meehan, Esq., of this place, admits that they accomplish a vast amount of damage, and also that it is not solely in quest of insects that they are attracted to the blossoms, but for the sake of the tender ovaries and ripened anthers. He says, "I have seen them attack the pear-tree within my father's nurseries, and scatter the blossoms in every direction. Even in the spring, I have known them to make terrible havoc upon the buds of the small shrubbery in the same locality."

That the luscious and highly-flavored raspberry is not free from the ravages of these birds, Mr. Anthony Strouse, of Chestnut Hill, is ready to testify. In a conversation with the writer, in the presence of several witnesses, he adds,—" During the past season (1877), I was compelled to destroy immense numbers of these birds, in order to save my fruit. At first, I was the friend of the sparrow, and built several houses for its accommodation. But its recent depredations have brought it into bad repute with me. A raid upon my grapes in the fall of 1876 paved the way for the proceedings which recent events have compelled me to institute against it. The luscious and juicy strawberry does not escape its ravages. Last June my neighbor's patch was entered and would have been entirely destroyed, had not necessity compelled him to cover the plants by netting stretched upon small upright posts in order to save the fruit, for which the birds showed considerable fondness."

Isaac Reiff, Esq., of Philadelphia, who has spent the most of his life within the limits of the city proper, and who has given considerable attention to the study of the habits of our birds, says, " Fewer birds visit the city squares and the sidewalks under sparrow rule, than formerly. Our native birds manifested less dread of the squirrels than of the sparrows. On the return of breeding period, many of our warblers and finches would stop in their migrations, and spend a few days in the heart of the city. Now, even on its outskirts, the merry chirp and agreeable warble are seldom heard."

George Wills, Esq., of Germantown, another informant, and a man of close observation and reliability, has devoted considerable attention to the study of the sparrow in its new home. He remarks, "Its insolent bearing towards our native birds, whenever the latter venture into occupied territories, combined with its lazy, idolent habits and destructive propensities, should be a sufficient inducement for the authorities to rescind the laws passed for its protection."

Other statements, equally as forcible and positive, could be given, until the accumulated evidence would cover hundreds of pages of closely printed matter, and all from persons of known probity who occupy high positions in this community, but the writer must forbear. Negativing the foregoing assertions, might be mentioned the observations of Philip Freas, editor of the "Germantown Telegraph," a weekly paper of moderate circulation), and those of John Bardsley, Esq., to whom must be attributed the honor of introducing the sparrows into Philadelphia. Mr. Freas has taken very little part in the discussion of the sparrow-question, but what he has said upon the subject is confined to a small article which appeared in his paper a few years ago. His remarks mostly related to personal observations upon his own premises. Substantially, he asserted that the sparrows did not molest or interfere in any way with our native birds, but dwelt upon the most intimate and friendly terms with them, sparrows, robins, and bluebirds building in close proximity to each other. Mr. Bardsley's interest in the sparrow must certainly be attributed to the part which he played in its introduction. It is, therefore, but natural that he should defend it against the attacks of its human enemies. Substantially, he says the sparrow is not more pugnacious than many of our native birds, the robin for example, and if so, it is mainly when actuated by amatory influences. Its destructive propensities are equalled, if not surpassed, by scores of indigenous species. It has certainly done much to rid our squares of the destructive canker-worm which made such terrible havoc upon the foliage of trees, and will continue to shower its blessings upon mankind wherever it shall spread. It is certainly an unmixed good.

Having adduced considerable evidence both for and against the sparrow, it now becomes the duty of the writer to weigh the matter carefully, thoughtfully, and thoroughly, and to assign it a place, according as its merits or demerits warrant, among either the beneficial or the injurious birds of this country. A special chapter will therefore be devoted to the consideration of this subject.

CHAPTER IV.

CONCLUDING REMARKS.

In Europe the sparrow has been placed by eminent and well-qualified investigators foremost in the rank of useful birds. When it has been exterminated, it has been necessary to re-establish and foster it at infinite trouble and expense. Over there it constitutes part and parcel of the natural economy of animal life; it has its place, and fills it.

It must not be vainly supposed that it is an unmixed good. Its destruction of the blossoms and fruits of trees, the tender flowers of herbaceous plants, and the ripened grain in rural districts, are facts too well known to be discredited, or passed silently by. Few writers upon the habits of this species seek to conceal its faults. But the destruction which it commits, although on a singularly grand scale, is nevertheless small, according to the concurrent testimony of reliable authorities, when contrasted with the immense benefits which accrue to agriculturists and fruit-growers in the destruction of millions of noxious insects in their various stages of development.

Judging from the rapid multiplication of the species, which, so far as I know, is unsurpassed by that of any other species of the *Fringillidæ*, it might be supposed that the supply of insect food would be largely disproportionate to the excessive demand, and, conse-

CONCLUDING REMARKS. 97

quently, a wholesale destruction of the farmer's crops would be the inevitable result. In every fauna left to itself, or but slightly disarranged by man, "a certain balance of forces is sooner or later established tending to the co-ordination and subordination of various forms of animal life."

Every species has a natural check to undue multiplication. When propagation has reached a certain limit, farther increase is stayed by natural conditions. Either the supply of food becomes diminished and thousands perish, the stronger alone surviving in the "struggle for existence," or else the overgrown species affords an extra allowance of food to its natural enemies which have waxed powerful enough to reduce the threatened numbers.

In America the birds exist under unnatural conditions. They are out of place. Their remarkable increase should not excite astonishment. Other instances than this could be cited to show the reaction of exotics upon the natural species. The Norway rat, which was introduced into this country many years ago, is destined to usurp the place of our native species. There are but few localities where the latter exists. Its hardy and pugnacious relative from the north of Europe, is slowly but surely supplanting it. Among plants, the white weed has overrun the entire country, and choked out native vegetation. Even the Indian, who once inhabited the whole of North America, is fast receding before the rapid advances of the energetic European, or his descendants.

The sparrow is rapidly exterminating the native songsters and insect-eating birds from our cities and large towns. Even in many rural districts the same condition of affairs has been unhappily brought about. These disastrous consequences will continue to follow the diffusion of the sparrows, unless means for prevention are taken. This species has no enemies, and consequently has nothing to fear. It is warmly domiciled, carefully fed, and sedulously encouraged to multiply. There is no natural check to its almost unlimited increase. If allowed to shift for itself, it is possible that the disturbed harmony might be re-adjusted in the long run, for nature is full of resources for all her emergencies.

We do not often give her the opportunity, but thwart and baffle her with the most determined pertinacity. It was only the other day that the shrikes (*Collurio borealis*) made their appearance upon Boston Common and began to decimate the ranks of the sparrows a little, when a crusade was instituted against them, by some person or persons who had the affair at his or their whimsical command. This was undoubtedly the first indication of a natural healthy reaction against the sparrows which has occurred, but it was most fatuitously nipped in the bud.

What would be the result if the sparrows were permitted to brave the seasons for themselves, and to seek their own subsistence as our own birds are compelled to do, it is difficult to imagine. At any rate, the special fostering of these birds by housing and victualling should be stopped. Let them be thrown upon their own resources, and take their chances with our smaller native birds, and see how they will fare.

Deprived of their daily allowances in the heart of large cities, where there is a scarcity of vegetable food-stuffs, it is probable that insect diet would be appropriated with a better *gusto*. Pressed by hunger, and in danger of starvation, during the famine winter months every nook and cranny would be searched for the lurking beetle, the hidden chrysalis, and the tiny egg. The fissured bark of trees would be probed, and the caitiffs within drawn from their resting-places with the bill. While some birds would remain in the city, amidst the scenes of past associations and pleasures, the greater part would doubtless find their way into the country, where seeds and insects are more plentiful. The happy results of this manner of treatment, both in the city and in the country, would be very apparent, on the return of the budding season, in the paucity of injurious insects. Besides, the habit of self-maintenance thus formed would continue to strengthen, and thousands of insects, during the seasons when these creatures run riot, would disappear before their voracious appetites. As an offset to this, it might be argued that this species is mainly granivorous, and consequently would do little towards holding in check the enemies of vegetation. Example after example might be given to show that animals of carnivorous habits readily adapt themselves to a vegetable diet, and others of herbivorous propensities, quite as easily become fitted to the digestion of animal food. Of course the appetite for vegetable diet would still continue amid all the vicissitudes of life. The "struggle for existence," during the predominance of the cold season, would act with telling effect upon the weaker portion of the community, the more powerful alone remaining to propagate the species on the return of warm weather. Flocking to the country in quest of food, they would doubtless become a prey to the shrike, which delights in rural districts. At any rate, a perceptible decrease in the amount of injuries committed would be apparent. But the compensating good which is experienced in Europe could never be attained, therefore it is highly probable that the amount of good accomplished would be more than balanced by the evil committed.

On the introduction of the sparrow into Philadelphia, which was about the time when nature was beginning to swarm with insect life, being a stranger in a strange land, it naturally took to eating indiscriminately everything that came within its reach. Insects, especially caterpillars of particular kinds, being very plentiful, and easily obtained, fell ready victims to its rapacious appetite. Horse-dung and street garbage eventually came in for a share of attention. In a brief time, on account of the eminent services which they had rendered in the destruction of that pest of vegetation, the canker-worm, this little creature had securely established itself in the public affection. Houses, both public and private, by the hundreds, some of the most costly architecture, began to appear in every direction. Charities poured in upon them from every source, and the gullible Philadelphian soon commenced to lavish more than usual attention upon these creatures of foreign extraction. The birds often fared much better than their poor human brethren. These fancied "saviors of vegetation" finally became well-housed and well-fed. Their good qualities were loudly applauded, and the law was constrained to throw around them its ægis of protection.

But a change soon came over the aspect of affairs. Too much pampering had engendered a spirit of laziness. Accustomed to an easy life, the birds assembled three times a day to receive their allowances of food. The results of such folly soon began to be apparent. The

CONCLUDING REMARKS. 101

squares became alive with caterpillars. The rusty vaporer crawled everywhere. Sparrows were never more plentiful. They abandoned their carnivorous propensities, in a great measure, and took to vegetable diet with a cheerful chirp. Their rural brethren soon followed suit. The sparrows should not be censured, for they merely obeyed the instincts of their nature. Necessity compelled them to insect diet.

In the spring, when plenty reigns supreme, they live at their ease, and in the most luxurious enjoyment. I can but repeat what I have iterated before. They are lazy pilferers, who set the unwholesome example of consuming what they do not earn. They should be colonized and sent back to England. If this plan is not practicable, take away from them the protection of the law, and let us have some return (we can never expect an equivalent) for the losses we have sustained. In England the peasantry are paid for potting them into sparrow-pies. Here no expense need be incurred. They can be made a source of revenue, as well as a sustainer of life.

From the evidence adduced in Chapters II. and III., being overwhelming in amount, and coming as it does from the most reliable authorities, there can be little doubt of the sparrow's utter uselessness. The testimony produced, of a negative character, is outweighed in quadruple proportion by that upon the opposite side. The small proportion of caterpillars destroyed, when contrasted with the waste and destruction of grains, blossoms, and fruits of various kinds, without reckoning the indirect injuries perpetrated in the expulsion of scores of highly insectivorous native species, must be apparent to every one who has given its history a careful and considerate attention. This nuisance, this destroyer of vegetation and pest of human society, deserves the censure of every honest and right-thinking individual, as well as the condemnation of the law.

A few remarks upon the motives which prompted the sparrow's introduction into this country, and also upon the propriety of such a course of action, cannot be deemed inappropriate, or misplaced. In treating this theme I must necessarily restrict what I have to say to facts brought within the sphere of personal observation, although other fields of research, outside of my immediate circle of vision, will receive considerable attention.

Let us now ask ourselves the question: What led to the sparrow's introduction? The answer thereto must certainly be apparent to the mind of every one who has kept his eyes open to his surroundings. For years antecedent to this event, the linden and other trees in our public squares and parks had been sorely infested by the span-worm, and other caterpillars of near and remote affinities, much to the disgust of pedestrians, and to the detriment of the trees. These, particularly the former, had multiplied to such an alarming extent, that they had become a downright public nuisance. The trees were literally filled with caterpillars, and thousands dangled from the ends of long silken threads into the faces of passers-by, or crawled their ugly lengths upon the forms of persons of delicate feelings and refined tastes.

In the midst of this unhappy state of things, the authorities, aroused somewhat from the lethargy into which they had fallen, began to revolve in their minds the expediency of getting rid of these pests and destroyers, and the means of accomplishing the desired object.

CONCLUDING REMARKS.

The experiment of introducing the sparrows had been tried in New York City, Boston, and elsewhere, with marked success. The ugly caterpillars had fast disappeared before the inveterate and persistent assaults of these courageous creatures. Nor is this success difficult of explanation. The sparrows were in a strange country, and almost entirely ignorant of its living flora, if we except a few plant species that are common to Europe and America. In municipal limits this diversity in plant-life is very conspicuous. With insect-life it is otherwise. Almost every tree has its particular occupants. While some afford nourishment to but a single species, others yield ample food for a dozen or more. The *Phalænidæ*, to which our numerous species of span-worms belong, are indiscriminate feeders. Hence, their presence in unlimited numbers wherever trees flaunt their foliage. Those who have studied this peculiar group of insects in their larval stages, know the perfect facility with which they can be identified. In general structure, the closest resemblance obtains between species, however remote the quarter of the globe in which they have been studied. It is evident from the above remarks that England can form no exception to the rule.

From these data, we reason that the sparrows were more or less familiar with this portion of our insect-fauna, and consequently manifested no fear of evil consequences resulting from the appropriation of such diet. Hence their attacks upon the canker-worm. These assaults would be the more vigorous in situations where there was a dearth of more desirable food. Thrown upon their own resources, nothing edible would be likely to escape their rapacity.

Immense hosts of insects were formerly destroyed by

these birds during the breeding-period, for the benefit of their young. There is reason to believe that nowadays the supply exceeds the demand. This is readily accounted for. Familiarity with their new home and its immense wealth of vegetable productions, has created in them a disgust for insects. Necessity alone drives them to such fare. Their wholesale destruction of the creeping caterpillar, more mobile imago, and less active chrysalis, during their early occupancy of this country, may be, in a great measure, attributed to the scarcity of other kinds of food, or to ignorance of the edible qualities of the same.

Perceiving the beneficial effects accomplished by these birds in other cities, is it at all surprising that the Philadelphian should see in them the saviors of vegetation, and the restorers of wonted confidence and ruined pleasure? Councils were besieged by men of influence and wealth, as though Nature had forgotten us in her distribution of avian existences, and the stupid blunder was committed of introducing these proverbial enemies of mankind.

Having briefly explained the motives which led to the commission of this shameful and unconsidered action, a few remarks upon the propriety of so doing cannot be deemed amiss. Were the sparrows needed? The condition of the squares and sidewalks in our large towns and cities, and the gradual destruction of the trees by insect pests, plainly spoke that something should be done, and that speedily, to remedy the constantly growing evil. Repeated efforts had been made to abate the nuisance. Scientific men had been appealed to, but their suggestions availed nothing. No remedy seeming likely to be offered, and the sparrow apparently accomplishing the task of holding the enemy in check, Philadelphia could do no more than follow the example of her sister cities.

A little knowledge, a little forethought as well as foresight, would have gone a great way towards solving the problem, and staying those proceedings which have caused the country to be overrun by these hardy, fearless creatures, which, by their ravages, are consuming our very substance—a thankless return for the many kindnesses and favors which they have received.

If our native species had been as carefully nourished as the sparrows have been, and been permitted to avail themselves of the protection of man by building unmolested in close proximity to his dwelling the same as they, the necessity for the sparrows would not have arisen. The law owed them a protection, but it refused to enforce it. If they took up their abode upon man's domains, their homes were desecrated, their treasures destroyed or fearfully mangled, and the parents themselves inhumanly sacrificed for no other cause than daring to defend their rightful property. Everybody seemed to fancy that he had an inborn right to wage incessant warfare against these happy creatures of the field and grove. Farmers, who should have protected them for services freely bestowed, became their most inveterate persecutors. The active kinglet, the warbling vireo, and the sturdy woodpecker, in their frequent visits to the blossoms and the bark of trees, for the insects and larvæ that lurked insidiously within, had been misjudged, and made to pay the penalty of death for their cleverness. This was undoubtedly an age of ignorance and superstition.

But times have changed. By the light of science,

our legislatures no longer grope in darkness. Wise and healthy laws have been enacted for the benefit of birds —those saviors of vegetation. And what has been the happy effects? These joyous creatures have forgotten their shyness, and now visit our yards and orchards, and repay our goodness by the destruction of myriads of vermin. To be sure they take a juicy berry occasionally, but then the vast amount of good which they accomplish, largely overbalances the mischief committed.

It is sufficiently obvious from all reports that a healthy condition of things is being produced in rural districts, and also in many of our large towns and cities that have not had their harmony disarranged by the much-to-be-detested sparrow. Had the city authorities, in laying out the plans of our large cities, reserved suitable plots of ground for the growth of shrubbery and trees, either within municipal limits or largely on the outskirts, these spots would have constituted, in course of time, available building-places for many of our smaller birds. From these coverts, as friendly relations became established with their human brethren, they would emerge to glean among the leaves of the trees which line our avenues, and occupy our lawns. The same object would undoubtedly have been gained had suitable gardens and lawns been attached to private as well as public buildings, and adorned with a profusion of vines and shrubbery. But this is acting on the presumption that these feathered creatures were under the protection of a stern and impartial law. But as most cities are now laid out, it is to be feared that the above project can never be satisfactorily carried into execution. As at present constituted, few native species could be found to be as accommodating as the sparrow. The robin, bluebird, wren, song and chipping sparrows, which are quite versatile in their habits, would, of all others, be the most likely to succeed.

If cities, like Philadelphia for example, that had entailed so much expense in providing comfortable homes for the squirrels, which certainly were of little use save to amuse children, and adults who had nothing else to do than to lounge about our squares, had taken as much interest in many of our smaller insectivorous birds, and encouraged their presence by every means that wisdom and judgment could devise, we should to-day not be pestered by these disgusting exotics, which seem destined to overspread the entire country, and drive our own native favorites away.

Westward the sparrows are slowly but surely directing their resistless course, like a baleful pestilence, sweeping everything before them, and leaving only ruin in their wake. All this has been brought about in less than twelve years. What another decade will accomplish, if these saucy knaves are permitted to go on as they have done, I do not venture to say. Their present depredations and odious practices give us a foretaste of what their future course of action will be. We shall be entirely deserted by our native-born feathered friends, and what of grains and fruits the sparrows do not take, will certainly be destroyed by the thousands of noxious insects, in their various developmental stages, which will then wantonly run riot. This will be the inevitable state of affairs. The trees will be stripped of their foliage even before they have flaunted their unfurled banners to the vernal breezes, and what will be the result? Despoiled of their respiratory organs, their mechanism will be clogged, and a long train of evils follow, ending in premature death.

The writer may be branded as a scientific zealot, carried away by imaginary fears. Be this as it may; he has a duty to perform, and manfully must he fulfil it. If he should shrink from its accomplishment, posterity will not hold him guiltless. Therefore, he must raise a voice of warning before the evil becomes so deep-rooted and widespread as to defy man's puny efforts to check it. He is no alarmist, but generally sees things as they exist. The handwriting upon the wall has been seen and recognized. The sparrows have been weighed in the balance, and found wanting. Their sins have been many and unpardonable. They will continue to increase and grow with each succeeding year. If anything is done, it should be done immediately. Now is the opportune moment. Now is the day of salvation. Let the law cease to protect them, and then let every one who has the good of his land and fellow-being at heart, strike till the last foe expires.

I am not alone in these opinions. Others have lifted their voices in condemnation of the nuisance. Abler men have discussed the uselessness of the sparrow. From every portion of the country which has yet been visited by these birds, we hear the same cry. Those who had at first befriended them, now clamor for their destruction. He who has kept his eyes open to his natural surroundings, cannot have failed to notice the impudence, pugnacity, rapacity, and destructiveness of these creatures. But how few, in comparison with the countless numbers of human beings who inhabit this continent, give the study of natural history a moment's consideration. They run their short race of life and enter the unknown, scarcely a whit wiser about natural phenomena than when they came into existence. They form an apt illustration of that class of beings who have eyes, but see not. Others, again, are excellent observers, but their minds are so warped by various prejudices and prepossessions, that their observations are unreliable and worthless. But the true scientific man has no predilections to sustain, no theories to save. He is a lover of truth for her own sake. The goddess, and not the altar upon which she sits enthroned, is, or ought to be, the object of his pious reverence. A few who pass for the genuine coin, I am sorry to say, are attracted by the gorgeousness of the shrine, and transfer their homage to an unsubstantial pageant. The American is behind his trans-Atlantic brother in matters of natural science. In Europe the masses are trained to be scientific observers. She has her scientific schools apart from her colleges and universities. Even her grammar schools are practised in this most essential branch of knowledge. Not so in America. In our colleges, with but few exceptions, other studies, the ancient languages for example, are given the prominence. Natural history holds a subordinate position. Our grammar schools, which have mainly to do with the masses, are too much crammed with the dry details of geography and history, to make room for the study of natural phenomena. Is it a wonder, then, that the average American should be so much inferior in the knowledge of such matters to the average European? With the cultivation of the observant and reflective faculties, arises this difference, and with the latter, an utter dislike for the humbler walks of literature. The imaginative faculties, from lack of proper nurture, would dwindle to reasonable proportions, and life would lose much of its poetry and romance. Consequently, the mind, no longer clogged by these enervating fetters, would grow to its full stature, and life be brought to a higher and nobler plane. A new era would then be ushered into existence—the millennium of scientific truth. May the day speed on swiftest pinions which will inaugurate this felicitous change.

Coming back from this digression to the subject-matter of discussion, the disreputable character of the sparrow is too well known to the candid and unbiassed observer, to leave in his mind any reasonable doubt. But if my readers have had neither the leisure nor the patience to examine into its life-history, I would respectfully solicit their careful perusal and earnest consideration of the innumerable facts which occur in Chapter II., and also of the corroborative evidence which is largely accumulated in the succeeding chapter. If they bring to the task a mind divested of preconceived opinions and national prejudices, they cannot help yielding assent to the following facts, which the writer holds to be incontrovertible:—

1. That in all localities which are cursed by the presence of sparrows, indubitable evidence exists of their extreme irritability and pugnacity.

2. That our smaller native species, the only rightful tenants of the soil, which have always been adequate to every emergency that has arisen, except in localities disarranged by human interference, are vigorously assailed and forced to flee before these irascible creatures.

3. That in situations which once afforded shelter and security to many of our insectivorous birds, the noisy

and disagreeable chatter of the sparrow is heard to the exclusion of the merry chirp and agreeable warble of our native songsters.

4. That its extraordinary salacity, the result of the overstimulated life which it leads, "rises to the dignity of a public scandal."

5. That, as the result of the special fostering which these birds have received, and are receiving, caterpillars are at a heavy discount, and blossoms, cherries, raspberries, strawberries, and grapes are eaten with a better gusto.

6. That when a sufficiency of boxes is not provided for nesting purposes, and there is a notable scarcity of ivied walls and decayed tree-hollows, cornices, window-caps, brackets, etc., are selected, and the nests deposited generally where they are most likely to be seen.

7. That in such localities they often become sources of considerable annoyance on account of their turbulence and droppings.

8. That their pilfering propensities, as shown by their daily raids upon the poultry-yards and pigeon-cotes, are unsurpassed for boldness by those of any other feathered species.

9. That for laziness and gluttony they stand unequalled, and set the unwholesome example of consuming what they do not earn.

10. That their grain-loving appetites frequently lead them into fields of standing and fallen wheat, where they commit, in many localities, untold ravages upon this staple sustainer of life, amounting, in some cases, to thousands of dollars' worth of loss.

www.ingramcontent.com/pod-product-compliance
Lightning Source LLC
Chambersburg PA
CBHW030407170426
43202CB00010B/1519